COMPUTERS AND COMPUTER APPLICATIONS IN DEVELOPING COUNTRIES

W0090622

Also by Ukandi G. Damachi

THEORIES OF MANAGEMENT AND THE EXECUTIVE IN
THE DEVELOPING WORLD
THE ROLE OF TRADE UNIONS IN DEVELOPING
SOCIETIES (*with Everett Kassalow*)
MANPOWER SUPPLY AND UTILIZATION IN GHANA,
NIGERIA AND SIERRA LEONE (*editor with Kodwo Ewusi*)
HUMAN RESOURCES AND AFRICAN DEVELOPMENT
(*with V. P. Diejomaoh*)
PUBLIC POLICY, INDUSTRIAL RELATIONS AND
EMPLOYMENT PROMOTION IN WEST AFRICA (*with
V. P. Diejomaoh*)
SOCIAL CHANGE AND ECONOMIC DEVELOPMENT IN
NIGERIA (*with Hans Dieter Seibel*)
INDUSTRIAL RELATIONS IN AFRICA (*with Hans Dieter
Seibel and Lester Trachtman*)
SELF-MANAGEMENT IN YUGOSLAVIA AND THE
DEVELOPING WORLD (*with Hans Dieter Seibel*)
SELF-HELP ORGANIZATIONS (*with Hans Dieter Seibel*)
MANAGEMENT PROBLEMS IN AFRICA (*with Hans Dieter
Seibel*)
FROM BLACK AFRICA
LEADERSHIP IDEOLOGY IN AFRICA: Attitudes Toward
Socio-Economic Development
THE ROLE OF TRADE UNIONS IN THE DEVELOPMENT
PROCESS: With a Case Study of Ghana
NIGERIAN MODERNIZATION: The Colonial Legacy
CREATING INDUSTRIAL PEACE IN NIGERIA
CONTEMPORARY PROBLEMS IN NIGERIAN
INDUSTRIAL RELATIONS (with Tayo Fashoyin)

Also by H. Ray Souder

SIMPLE LINEAR AND MULTIPLE REGRESSION
ANALYSIS

Computers and Computer Applications in Developing Countries

Edited by

Ukandi G. Damachi

Professor and Dean, Faculty of Business Administration
University of Lagos

H. Ray Souder

Associate Professor of Management
University of Central Florida

and

Nicholas A. Damachi

Adjunct Associate Professor of Industrial Engineering
University of Cincinnati

MACMILLAN
PRESS

First published 1987

Published by
THE MACMILLAN PRESS LTD
Houndmills, Basingstoke, Hampshire RG21 2XS
and London
Companies and representatives
throughout the world

British Library Cataloguing in Publication Data
Computers and computer applications in
developing countries.
1.   Electronic digital computers —
Developing countries
I.   Damachi, Ukandi Godwin   II. Souder,
H. Ray   III. Damachi, Nicholas A.
004'.09172'4   QA76.5

ISBN 978-0-333-41383-8   ISBN 978-1-349-08647-4 (eBook)
DOI 10.1007/978-1-349-08647-4

To
Mr Justin Jabekong Damachi
Mrs Justina Lami Damachi
Mrs Luella Goering
Mr William Goering (deceased)

Contents

Preface

In view of current technological advances, a major issue that deserves consideration is to determine what role automation may play in the development process in developing nations. One approach to evaluate the role would be to delineate the goals of development, assess the present or existing conditions as well as available resources in the developing nations, then formulate a strategy for implementation that would facilitate the movement from the existing developing state to the desired conditions established by development objectives.

The role of automation may be assessed by examining its potential in facilitating the attainment of development objectives. While this conceptualisation may neglect some practical problems involved in development efforts, it does provide a framework for examining the development process and how it may be impacted by automation.

The ultimate goal of development efforts in any developing country encompasses a desire to stir that country into a 'developed' state. This implies, among other things, that the country must develop the capabilities to become very productive; thereby improving the standard of living of its people, establishing an industrial and technological base, and becoming competitive in the world market place. Productivity improvement and growth underlie such a process, and are vital to the long-term survival of developing countries; and even developed nations. If developing nations are to capture a share of the world markets, competitive pressures demand that these countries produce goods and services of such quality that they can compete favourably in the international markets, and are not merely limited to domestic use. Manufacturing of goods of acceptable quality by developing nations becomes even more crucial if they must reduce the level of importation products which tends to erode their scarce foreign exchange reserves and cause trade deficits to mount. The need for improved productivity in developing nations must be underscored. It is through productivity gains that these countries can create jobs by increasing the demand for the output of their economies, create more real per capita income, which improves the standard of living of their people, stimulate a favourable trade balance with other countries, and gain control of inflation. A typical approach to productivity enhancement in developing nations involves emphasis on the utilisation of locally available resources.

One of the dominant features of many developing nations is an availability of surplus labour and unemployment. In view of this, proponents of appropriate technology advocate the choice and use of labor-intensive technology and techniques to take advantage of the available excessive labour and reduce the levels of unemployment. While there may be some benefits provided by this approach, its viability as an appropriate long-term development strategy for developing countries that are at the threshold of an economic takeoff is suspect. Some of the reasons advanced against the utilisation of labour-intensive technology are thus: first, workable technologies that employ more labour are not available; second, labour-intensive technology usually results in a loss of productivity and production, and often in a loss of export sales; third, often the institutional arrangements and control necessary to police the efforts are cumbersome, bureaucratic, and hard to implement. This in turn often leads to discrimination against investment, which may negate the increased employment achieved through the use of labour-intensive technology. At this point, a distinction must be made between those developing countries which are poised for an economic takeoff and those that are not. The heterogeneity of developing countries compels this distinction. The choice of automation may not be suited to the very low income countries. However, for those countries with adequate resources for an economic takeoff, the role of automation deserves closer examination.

The ability is questionable of goods produced using labour-intensive technology, fraught with quality problems, to compete in international markets. The move toward a competitive posture and efforts to gain a share of the world markets demand that developing nations recognise that technological know-how is basic to a nation's economic development. They should therefore closely examine the adoption of automation and mechanisation in areas that include manufacturing, agriculture, and process industries.

Historically, improvements in output levels, improved quality levels, mass production, and overall productivity improvements have been attained through increasing levels of automation and mechanisation. At present, there is a continuing trend toward increased automation in the industrialised world, thus, underscoring the importance of automation in improving productivity and maintaining a competitive edge. The emerging trend is computer-integrated manufacturing, flexible manufacturing systems, computer-aided design, material resource planning, robotics and a host of other computer-oriented support systems. The case for automation appears to be strong, and suggests that developing nations that are ready for more rapid advancement should consider it as an instrument for development.

A policy formulation that adopts automation as a major instrument of development would provide the leadership of developing nations with a direction for the future. It should also provide framework for making decisions about resource allocation, developing manpower equipped with requisite technical and computer skills – since computer technology is an integral part of automation – and developing competent managers to manage complex computer-based production systems. In short, initial efforts should focus on developing the skills as well as the administrative and management procedures that underpin computer technology.

There are, undoubtedly, some sceptics regarding an automation approach to development. However, the potential benefits of a properly conceived plan for automation in developing nations as a means to progress merits close scrutiny.

While there is considerable debate and a growing focus on the role of automation in the development process, it has rather been limited by the number of active participants. This stems from the general lack of awareness and understanding in developing nations of computers, their capabilities and role as a major component of automation. This book presents a plethora of information on computers in one readable and easy to understand volume. It is geared to creating an awareness and understanding of computers by people in the developing world and provides a wide range of computer applications. It sensitises managers in the third world to the viability of computer technology as a tool to both improve productive output and boost economic returns. I hope that this book will stimulate enthusiasm to use computers.

Because of the pioneering nature of this work on the application of computers in the developing world, the book requires input from several contributors. Also, because there are very many diverse interests in the uses of the computer in the developing countries, this book has had to draw on the many talents of international scholars who are interested in applying the computer to the problems of the development process. Two of the editors of this book, Nicholas Damachi and H. Ray Souder, are already planning to go a step further after this initial effort. Both authors intend to look at the next level after they observe how this book is received.

Among the business community in developing countries; the international business community; academia, and government, the debate concerning the use of automation and industrialisation as a means of development is becoming quite interesting and deserves the attention of scholars interested in this process. The two editors are interested in examining this controversy more closely and coming out with some good policy considerations which will aid the rapid industrialisation of the third world countries which are on the threshold for an economic surge.

UKANDI G. DAMACHI

Acknowledgements

The editors would like to acknowledge the following people for contributing in one way or another to this book: Andrew A. Agom, Funke Adenuga, Javeed Khadervelli Ahmed, Lakeitha Copeland, Dympna Damachi, Franca Damachi, Nkoyo Essien, Jennifer D. Harris, Maria A. Igberaese, Lucy Damachi Itam, Deborah Jones, Velta M. Kelly, Aderenle Latoma, Anthony Meldahl, Diane Mitchell, Aguzie Sociis Okolie, Kemi Soyode, Brenda D. Tillery and Francis Akpak Unyi. Thanks also to Ginny Shell.

U. G. D.

Notes on the Contributors

Mohammed E. Bayou is an Assistant Professor of Accounting at Xavier University, Cincinnati, Ohio USA. Dr Bayou received his Msc in Accounting from the University of Winsconsin and MBA and PhD degree in Accounting from the University of Cincinnati. He is a member of the American Accounting Association; the sections of Management Accounting and International Accounting; and a Management Accounting Cordinator for the National Association of Accountants. He has taught at several universities including Miami University, Oxford, Ohio; and Northern Kentucky University (NKU) Highland Heights; Kentucky. He has served as a Consultant for the small Business Development Centre at NKU; and has published in the Woman CPA and Business Review Journals.

Michael E. Doherty is an Analytics Specialist in the Management Systems Division of Procter & Gamble, which he joined in 1975. He received a BS in Physics from Xavier University in 1968 and the PhD in Computer and Information Science from the Ohio State University in 1974. His interests include large scale combinatorial optimisation, decision analysis, and artificial intelligence. He is an adjunct associate professor in the Department of Quantitative Analysis & Information Systems at the University of Cincinnati.

Michael C. Berry is an Admissions Counsellor and Cooperating Lecturer in English at Northern Kentucky University. He previously held the position of Special Lecturer in English and worked extensively teaching English for Special Purposes courses to international businesspersons. He has also served as a business communications consultant to various businesses and agencies. Prior to this, he taught English at the University of Cincinnati, Cincinnati, Ohio. He is the author of short stories and scholarly articles.

Jagtar Chaudhry is a Research Scientist with the Institute of Advanced Manufacturing Sciences (IAMS). Previously, he was a Systems Manager of AA Data Systems Inc. Cincinnati, Ohio USA. He received his BSc degree in Electrical Engineering (1980) from the Institute of Technology, Banris Hindu University, India. He obtained his MSc in Electrical and Computer Engineering in 1983 from the University of Cincinnati. He is a member of the Institute of

Electrical and Electronic Engineers: Association of Computing Machinery; and the Institute of Industrial Engineers. His main areas of interest are system software, industrial engineering and business applications. He has extensive experience in micro and minicomputer systems and has been studying closely present and future trends in computer hardware and software.

Nicholas A. Damachi is General Manager of Lamic Nigeria Ltd and adjunct Associate Professor in the Department of Mechanical and Industrial Engineering at the University of Cincinnati, USA. Dr Damachi has served as consultant to a number of private organizations and worked as systems engineer with the technical services group, Division of Water, City of Columbus. His areas of interest include computer/information systems analysis and design, applied operations research and statistics, water utility systems, productivity enhancement, as well as the practice of industrial engineering in developing nations. He has published in these and other areas. Dr Damachi is a member of the Institute of Industrial Engineers, Xigma Xi, and Alpha Pi Mu.

Ukandi G. Damachi is Professor and Dean of the Faculty of Business Administration at the University of Lagos. His previous publications include *Theories of Management and the Executive in the Developing World*; *The Role of Trade Unions in Developing Societies* (with Everett Kassalow; *Manpower Supply and Utilization in Ghana, Nigeria and Sierra Leone* (editor with Kodwo Ewusi); *Human Resources and African Development* (with V. P. Diejomaoh); *Public Policy, Industrial Relations and Employment Promotion in West Africa* (with V. P. Diejomaoh); *Social Change and Economic Development in Nigeria* (with Hans Dieter Seibel); *Industrial Relations in Africa* (with Hans Dieter Seibel and Lester Trachtman); *Self-Management in Yugoslavia and the Developing World* (with Hans Dieter Seibel); *Self-Help Organizations* (with Hans Dieter Seibel); and *Management Problems in Africa* (with Hans Dieter Seibel).

Sudesh Duggal is Associate Professor of Information Systems at Northern Kentucky University. His teaching emphasis is on the introductory information systems courses, computer programming courses, and systems analysis and design courses. He is currently completing requirements for his doctorate degree and devoting attention to developing the systems analysis and design and data base management courses. He has several years' consulting experience to apply to his teaching.

William Holloway is a graduate of Baker University and the Graduate School of the University of Cincinnati. He has been a production manager for Hallmark Cards, Inc. and has thirteen years experience as a salesman, sales trainer, and sales manager for the Gillette Co. He has nine years experience as a management consultant working with a number of United States Fortune 500 companies and five state governments. Currently he is Associate Professor of Management at Northern Kentucky University.

William Leigh is an Associate Professor of Computer Science at the University of Southern Mississippi. He has held various positions with major corporations including IBM, Ambulatory Patient Care, Inc. and Data Methods Corporation. Dr Leigh's research interests include quantitative methods applications, decision-making, expert systems, and systems design. He has published in these and other areas. His most recent book is *Programming Business Systems with Basic*.

William Lindsay is Professor of Management and Chairman of the Management and Marketing Department at Northern Kentucky University. Dr Lindsay has held positions in industrial engineering and planning with E. I. Dupont, Southern Airways and the Department of Defense. During the past several years, he has served as an engineering and management consultant to government and industrial organizations. Dr Lindsay has written numerous papers and articles on strategic management, quality and operations management. He is a member of the Academy of Management, the Institute of Industrial Engineers, the American Institute for Decision Sciences and the International Association for Quality Circles.

O. Geoffrey Okogbaa is an Assistant Professor of Industrial Engineering in the Mechanical and Industrial Engineering Department at the University of Cincinnati. Dr Okogbaa's research interests are in the areas of modelling and simulation of human-machine systems, flexible manufacturing systems, applied statistics and industrial engineering applications in developing nations. Dr Okogbaa has authored and co-authored several publications for professional journals. He is a senior member of IIE, a member of Alpha Pi Mu, Texnikoi, and an active member of the Cincinnati chapter of IIE.

Jan Prickett is Assistant Professor of Information Systems at Northern Kentucky University, Highland Heights, Kentucky. He received his Ph.D. from the University of Kentucky, Lexington, Kentucky. Dr Prickett currently teaches computer-related courses in the College of Business at Northern Kentucky University. He serves as a member of two committees (Tracking and Evaluation Committee; 1985 ISECON Executive Committee) of the Education Foundation, Data Processing Management Association.

Richard L. Shell is Professor and Director of Industrial Engineering in the Department of Mechanical and Industrial Engineering at the University of Cincinnati. In addition, Dr Shell is presently Technical Director for the Institute of Advanced Manufacturing Sciences, a nonprofit corporation designed as a joint enterprise incorporating industry, local and state government, and the University of Cincinnati to foster manufacturing research, development and technology transfer. Dr Shell's past business experience has included engineering and management positions with Bourns, Ampex, and IBM. During the past several years, he has served as an engineering and management consultant for government and private industry. He is presently serving as a board of directors member for several corporations.

H. Ray Souder is Associate Professor of Management at the University of Central Florida. He was an Assistant Professor of Computer Information Systems at Northern Kentucky University. He has held various executive positions in several corporations and has worked as a consultant for government and private industry. Dr Souder's research and consulting interests include quantitative methods applications, decision support systems, database, and management. He has published in these and other areas.

Rick D. Stuart is a graduate of the University of Cincinnati and is currently the Assistant to the Director for Academic Computing and a Lecturer in Information and Decision Sciences at Xavier University. Prior to his present position Mr Stuart was the department chairman in charge of computing studies at Southwestern College of Business as well as having experience as an independent research consultant. In addition to his regular duties Mr Stuart is also a member of the Data Processing Management Association's National Model Curriculum Committee for 1984, a contributor to *Educational Technology* and a member of the Digital Equipment Corporation Users Society.

1 Computers and Developing Nations

Nicholas A. Damachi and H. Ray Souder

1.1 INTRODUCTION

The world grows smaller. The world's marketplaces are closer together. Due to advances in transportation, open trading, technology transfer, and research and development, computers will soon be available in large quantities for utilisation by business managers and professionals of developing nations. The primary challenge that this technological reality presents is, 'Will these managers be prepared for technological changes in how business is conducted?' This question requires an in-depth analysis to provide proper answers. A starting point from which to answer this question would be to examine existing computer installations and their utilisation in developing nations.

The existing level of computer utilisation varies among developing nations, however, at present, there appears to be a lag in the overall substantive use of computers in these countries. On the other hand, computers and computer technology have become an integral part of the way of life in developed nations and their capabilities, importance and limitations are well understood. The seminal role of computers in enhancing operations and decision-making in government, education, manufacturing and service industries is well documented. Computer technology has made significant contributions to the attainment of higher standards of living, improved health care, faster communications, more efficient operations and overall productivity improvements in the developed world.

1.2 POTENTIAL APPLICATIONS

An examination of prevailing conditions in many developing nations reveals that enormous potential exists for the application of computer technology in business, government, industry, commerce, education and service industries. Careful design of these systems coupled with

1

modest and selective application of computers in some phases of operations will enhance the managerial process. Also, with creativity in systems design that takes advantage of the networking capabilities of today's small computers, thus permitting multiple terminal/users, many technical and business applications can be built around mini-computers. As a result, with limited capital resources, an awesome amount of computer power can be relatively inexpensively acquired that can be used for a wide range of business and technical applications. Managers, by allowing computers to make routine decisions traditionally made by themselves, will be able to devote more time to the planning function.

The low cost, flexibility, and wide range of applications of small computers of today deserve emphasis. There are small computer systems currently available for a cost less than the annual cost of one clerical worker (Shell and Damachi, 1984). Cost no longer precludes use of computers by small or medium-sized businesses. The features of low cost, flexibility, and wide range applications are of tremendous value and justify computer applications in developing nations. The productive capacity of a business or government establishment can be greatly extended by the utilisation of small computer systems.

In many developing countries, government establishments are among the largest employers. In these organizations, data processing is performed manually. Functions such as payroll, accounting, planning, management information generation and reporting, budgeting, personnel records, and inventory control require a tremendous number of labour hours. Numerous business and other service industry functions are also performed manually. Data processing in banking services, for instance, begs for computerisation in many nations. Such problems as long waiting lines, human errors in calculations, and inadequate systems for generating management information could all be addressed with automation.

In general, manual operations are slow, may be inaccurate, and are costly when the amount of data involved is moderate to large. Manual data processing operations are susceptible to human error through carelessness, illness, and boredom and are of course limited by the speed of the human hand and eye. Organisations such as loan agencies, manufacturers, trucking companies, insurance companies, and sales agencies can all benefit from the data processing capabilities of computers. These include functions such as accounts receivable, and payable, invoice preparation, marketing data, records and forecast, and reviewing customer profiles and creditworthiness (Silver and Silver 1977).

1.3 IMPEDIMENTS TO COMPUTER UTILISATION IN DEVELOPING NATIONS

A number of factors contribute to the low degree of computer utilisation in developing nations. A fundamental underlying factor is a general lack of knowledge about the role and use of computers by managers, administrators, policy-makers, some engineers and other professionals, and government executives. Lack of awareness by these key individuals of the role, capacity, capabilities, and limitations of computers and data processing impedes their use in government agencies, schools, hospitals, banking, transportation and other businesses which could benefit from using computer technology.

There are managers and administrators in developing nations who hold views that computer technology can be productively utilised only in the developed nations. In addition, it has been suggested that existing conditions in developing nations are not conducive to the use of computer systems. Some reasons offered for hesitance, or outright unwillingness to adopt computers include:

1. Lack of adequate and uninterrupted power supply; surges and drops in power voltages.
2. Lack of properly trained computer and technical support staff.
3. Lack of funds for computer system acquisition, improvement and expansion; pervading notions that computers are expensive and hard currency required to buy or lease them cuts into limited available foreign exchange.
4. Lack of belief in computer technology; preference for manual operations; resistance to change and innovation.
5. Concern over computer security.
6. Problems experienced by existing computer installations tend to support notions that most computers cannot be productively integrated into the work environment, i.e., they are under-utilised and are operated less than three hours per day, in some instances.
7. Scepticism about word processing capabilities of computers.
8. Computer applications not geared to immediate needs of management in developing nations. (Taylor and Obudho, 1977)

Some of these reasons of course, tend to reveal a lack of awareness or familiarity with developments in the computer field. As mentioned previously, the cost of modern computer systems has fallen drastically, while their power, speed and capabilities have risen sharply; thus enhancing their cost justification and applications.

General purpose computers may be operated with small electricity generating sets. In some developing nations with power supply problems, success has been demonstrated using anti-mains-electricity failure operating systems, whereby generating sets automatically start and take only seconds for an electrical device to switch over after the loss of major power supply. In general, there are computer systems currently available that are simple to install and use, requiring no special wiring. They provide the operator total control and are user friendly.

Overall, some of the reasons offered for the non-use of computers in developing nations have been rendered less significant by developments in computer technology. In the view of the authors, the major impediment to the utilisation of computers in these countries is inadequate appreciation, awareness and understanding of the potential and capabilities of computers by management, resistance to innovation and change from existing modes of operation and decision-making. One approach for the enhancement of computer usage is to develop an understanding of computers and an appreciation of the kinds of operations that they can perform. Such an understanding will foster a belief in computer technology, eliminate some misconceptions, scepticism and concern about computers, and may generate management enthusiasm for their use. This may bring about the allocation of resources for computer systems acquisition and improvements by management. In doing this, the developing nations can learn from the computerisation implementation experience and mistakes of the industrialised countries.

1.4   LESSONS FROM DEVELOPED COUNTRIES

Part of the lesson provided by the computerisation experience of industrialised countries includes the need to dispel the notion that computers eliminate jobs. This notion, widely held in developing nations, and in view of the unemployment and underemployment problems of developing nations, appears to be one of the major factors impeding the rate of computer adoption. Judged by the experience of developed nations, the introduction of computers into factories, for instance, appears to eliminate routine and low-level jobs. However, there appears to be a net increase in employment during the initial phases of computerisation. The major impact is a shift from direct labour workforce to indirect labour jobs. These have a higher technology content, and require new types of worker, including computer operators, programmers, maintenance personnel, and technical support staff. The introduction of computers in the office tends to upgrade the skill requirements needed (Fite 1965). Other lessons that can be derived from the computerisation experience of industrialised nations include:

1. Changes in organisational structure and procedures that must result, in order to benefit from applying a new technology such as the computer. Minimal benefits result by merely converting existing and mechanised procedures to a computer without fundamental redesign.
2. Computer installation costs are generally underestimated, due to poor project planning and control, poor selection of leadership and technical personnel; failure of top management to appreciate the difficulties; and overreliance on vendor promises. Benefits are generally overestimated as a result of the lack of commitment on the part of computer information users to effect changes in established but ineffective procedures and the lack of top management involvement to assure that promised changes are implemented.
3. The selection and installation of computers is generally hastily done, and they lie underutilised for long periods due to poor data processing personnel selection and training; long lead time in the development of systems; poor selection of application made without sufficiently consulting operational staff on the organisational changes that must be made before the benefits of computerisation can occur. (Taylor and Obudho 1977, Fite 1965)

If developing nations are to take advantage of the enormous potential offered by computer technology, then top executives, managers and business professionals should develop a commitment to computerisation. They are the ones who possess the knowledge, authority and responsibility to plan and institute broad changes in their organisations. The extent to which computer technology is productively utilised would depend upon their willingness to commit resources to train personnel with required technical skills. While some extent of system analysis is required prior to computerisation, there are small computer systems currently available which may be cost-justified for a single application, and do not require extensive systems work prior to their use. In addition, individual workers may improve their work performance and output through the personal use of a computer.

Although, new computer systems are user-friendly, the need to persuade workers in developing nations to accept and use these new tools cannot be overemphasised. The ability of managers and professionals to overcome resistance to change and to make meaningful use of the technology is paramount. Worker involvement in the effort to computerise is a powerful tool that could assist in overcoming resistance to change.

The lack of understanding of the role of computers in some organisations has created problems for some existing installations. Some top management policies and guidelines require that funds generated by the computer department be turned over to central administration. As a result, the managers of computer installations do not always have control over the funds they generate. On the other hand, there is much unwillingness on the part of central administration to allocate funds to the computer installations for much needed system maintenance, and acquisition of new and improved systems. Management simply views the computer department as an income-producing centre. Consequently, computer system managers are faced with old equipment, with frequent breakdowns and unavailability of expensive spare parts. Such problems can be alleviated if top management is made aware of the increased economic benefits provided by computers, the data analysis and processing capabilities they provide, and the need for system maintenance and upgrading of equipment.

1.5 CENTRALISED VERSUS DECENTRALISED COMPUTER SYSTEMS

In the past, as a result of a proliferation of small computers in government deparments of some developing nations, centralising computer facilities was thought to be essential. Wallace (1977) captures the arguments offered by government electronic data processing (EDP) managers for centralising computer facilities. They are:

1. Many small computers are less cost-effective than a few large computers.

2. A single large computer installation can effect other economies of scale in terms of documentation, productivity standards, and specialisation of personnel.
3. A large computer is not only more cost-effective, but also more flexible.
4. A central bureau can develop systems across ministerial lines to reduce duplication of effort and increase standardisation of collection and reporting.

The arguments against centralisation frequently offered by computer vendors who are anxious to protect their customer base are that a large sophisticated computer requires more sophisticated technical and management personnel (often expatriate); that computers in government data processing do not necessarily exhibit significant economies of scale; that a central computer bureau is likely to be unresponsive to a variety of users; and that coordination and priority-setting mechanisms for allocating computer resources among users are lacking. In the past, computer systems were built around inflexible large mainframe computers, a practice which today is no longer a limiting factor.

The centralisation/decentralisation issue has been obviated by the networking capabilities of currently available, low cost micro and minicomputers. However, early poor experiences with the use of computers continues to hinder increased use. While advances in computer technology have increased the power and capabilities of smaller computers, and enhanced their viability in developing countries, the serious problem of inaccuracy of input data remains. Wallace states that, 'input accuracy is a symptom that underlies the entire formulation of computer use in developing countries, and independent software firms and private service bureaus are vital resources for correcting problems created by the aggressive marketing policies of the major computer hardware vendors'.

1.6 SYSTEMS ANALYSTS ISSUES AND PROBLEMS

The lack both of system analysts of professional calibre, and of demand from managers has contributed to the absence of sophisticated computer applications. There are pitfalls associated with computer training that is limited to the training of clients' programmers by computer vendors. Wallace (1977) puts the need for systems analysts and associated problems in focus after examining cases of computer use:

> heavy reliance on vendor designed courses by developing countries for systems analysts tends to develop systems analysts whose only skills lie in solving problems by putting them on a computer. As a result, managers faced with clerical and administrative problems have no other type of technician. Consequently, a developing country that experiences a shortage of systems analysts should train its personnel in a variety of systems skills, for instance, work study, incentive pay systems, methods study, forms design, and clerical training.

Systems analysis and design courses offered by computer vendors, typically only present the tools necessary to computerise a system. These courses appear to ignore alternative problem-solving techniques, and following analysis of a problem, the analyst is required only to design a system using a computer. To successfully and productively integrate the computer into the work environment, the manager in a developing country needs to be aware of this proclivity, and to bear it in mind when making decisions to purchase.

An example of a systems analysis course offered by computer vendors in developing nations requires two weeks and consists of the following topics (Wallace, 1977):

> interviewing, identifying information flows and recording files and documents of the present system; presenting the results of the study; analysing the objectives of the system and needs of the users; preparing statement of user requirements of a proposed system.

The systems design course starts where the systems analysis course leaves off and requires three weeks. Typical areas include:

> constructing a computer systems flow chart and describing the processing steps; drawing procedural flow charts for the associated clerical functions; listing the data in proposed files and describing the method of access; designing the output records and input forms; and preparing program specification.

A United Nations report (1971) on the application of computer technology for development also issued some caution on the dependence on the training packages of equipment suppliers. The report recommends that governments of developing countries should formulate national policies that address both short-term and long-term objectives based on considerations of local control of technology transfer and local suppliers of technology, scarcity of skilled manpower and foreign exchange, and job creation problems. The policy encourages computer application only where national benefits are assured. Education policies should be designed by the government to produce a proper mix of computer professionals, decision makers trained in the advantages and disadvantages of computers and non-computer professionals who can use computers to enhance their productivity.

1.7 PHILOSOPHY OF THE BOOK

This book aims at developing or enhancing the understanding of computers by managers, administrators, students and professionals in government, business and academia in the developing nations through explanations and descriptions of the basics of computer technology and a discussion of potential application areas. In pursuit of this objective, it focuses on the problems of developing nations which typically include poor management, work practices that are labour-intensive, inefficient and ineffective and low productivity (Shell and Damachi, 1980). It explains the computer capabilities currently available and their wide range of applications. It views the computer as a proven tool for productivity enhancement, and provision of economic benefits. Computers make possible certain types of data analysis, and routinise some tasks that would otherwise be impossible to perform. This book integrates computers and computer technology and the problems of developing nations into a framework that will assist the managers and professionals in developing nations to recognise the role of the computer in the problems they face, and how computers facilitate problem-solving and management. This philosophy is illustrated by Figure 1.1. In view of the rapid changes in computer technology, this book adopts a forward looking posture to acquaint the manager or professional in the developing world, with changes to expect in the future, in order to minimise a feeling of obsolescence.

In developing nations, although data processing managers and personnel might have some experience, albeit usually with older computer hardware systems, the average manager does not even possess this experience. Their understanding of computers is so

Figure 1.1   Philosophy of the book

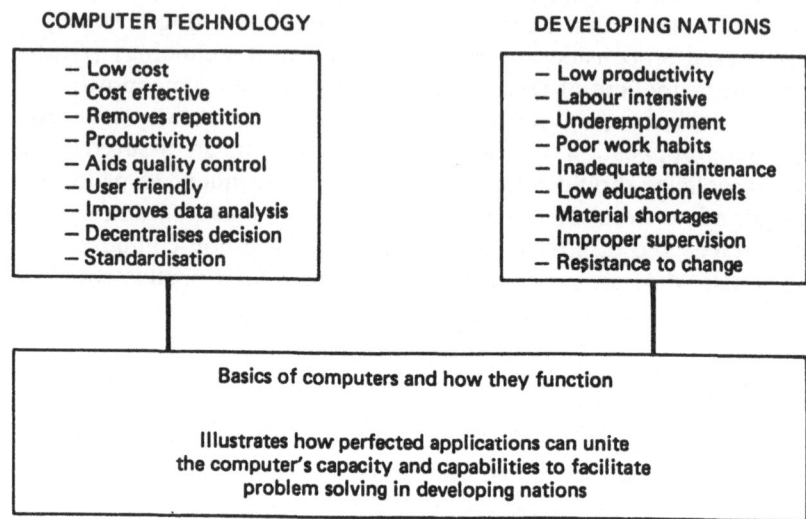

COMPUTER TECHNOLOGY

- Low cost
- Cost effective
- Removes repetition
- Productivity tool
- Aids quality control
- User friendly
- Improves data analysis
- Decentralises decision
- Standardisation

DEVELOPING NATIONS

- Low productivity
- Labour intensive
- Underemployment
- Poor work habits
- Inadequate maintenance
- Low education levels
- Material shortages
- Improper supervision
- Resistance to change

Basics of computers and how they function

Illustrates how perfected applications can unite
the computer's capacity and capabilities to facilitate
problem solving in developing nations

negligible that they would not be able to even begin to discuss computer utilisation. This book is intended to introduce managers to the basics of computers, and to enable them to make intelligent decisions about integrating them into their work environment. Certain caveats should be stated. Managers should be made aware of the need for proper and sound systems analysis *prior to* computerisation, and consequently the appropriateness of developing systems analysis skills within their organisations.

1.8   ORGANISATION OF THE BOOK

The book is organised in the following order of presentation. Chapters 2 through 5 are written to give the reader an overview of data processing, computers, computer terminology, and an integrative understanding of computer concepts. Chapter 2 discusses data processing and its role in the firm's organisation, and how the individual professional can best utilise processed data. Chapter 3 describes computer hardware, i.e., equipment, its functions, and how data processing is achieved using the hardware. Chapter 4 addresses computer programs – known as software – and their development and utilisation. Chapter 5 provides an overview of the historical development of programming languages and explains the various software systems for different applications such as operating systems, graphics and manufacturing.

Chapter 6 discusses integrating technology into strategic planning One, if not the primary, benefit of using the computer is that because routine functions are handled with ease the professional has more time to plan. This chapter also presents a systematic approach to strategic planning and how an organisation can best utilise this systematic approach supported by technology.

Chapters 7 to 10 discuss the various applications the professional can utilise with and on the computer. Chapter 7 looks at the accounting function and how the computer has improved the manager's task while using up-to-date financial and managerial data. Chapter 8 discusses service industry uses of the computer in today's work environment. Service industry applications are growing at a very rapid rate and with more data available the need to evaluate becomes essential.

Chapters 9 and 10 present excellent overviews of database and decision support systems and the composition of text. Most people when thinking of computers think about numbers and forget that data can also comprise letters and symbols. Databases and decision support systems are the newest state-of-the-art applications available today.

Finally, chapter 11 looks into the future and presents various issues that are associated with computers, work productivity, and how different jobs may be modified because of technology.

This book is written for business managers and other professionals in developing nations. From the knowledge and experience of the authors and the contributors, there is a need for a quality publication that can accurately introduce computers and their utilisation to a group of professionals whose needs are different. Due to the international backgrounds and expertise of the authors and contributors it is felt that there is an excellent understanding of the needs of developing nations and of how computers can best be utilised to assist in meeting those needs.

How to best use this book is an important factor to those professionals who purchase it. The book should first be considered as an excellent introduction to the basics of computers, computer concepts, and their applications in a professional work environment. Secondly, and equally important is the utilisation of the book as a reference.

1.9 SUMMARY

Enormous potential exists for the application of computer technology in developing nations. The rate of computerisation is however impeded by a lack of understanding of computers, their capabilities and the type of operations they can perform, together with host of other misconceptions. The viability of computer usage in developing nations is enhanced by the flexibility, low capital and operating costs, and wide range of business and technical applications of today's small computers. In using computers, the developing nations can learn and benefit from the computerisation experience and mistakes of the industrialised nations.

References

DAMACHI, U. G.(1970) *Nigerian Modernization: The Colonial Legacy* (New York: The Third Press).

DAMACHI, U. G. (1978) *Theories of Management and the Executive in the Developing World* (London: Macmillan).

FITE, H. H. (1965) *The Computer Challenge to Urban Planner and Administrators* (New York: Spartan Books).

HEARLE, E., and MASON, R. J. (1963) *A Data Processing System for State and Local Governments* (Englewood Cliffs, New Jersey: Prentice-Hall).

SHELL, R. L., and DAMACHI, N. A. (1980) 'Managing the Industrial Engineering Function in Developing Countries: The Role of the IE', *Institute of Industrial Engineering Annual Conference Proceedings*.

SHELL, R. L., and DAMACHI, N. A. (February, 1984) 'Improving Water Utility Management', *Water Engineering and Management*.

SILVER, G. A., and SILVER, J. B., (1977) *Data Processing for Business* (New York: Harcourt Brace Jovanovich).

SOUDER, H. R., and DAMACHI, N. A. (1986) 'Introduction of Computers to Management in Developing Countries', in Damachi, U. G. and Seibel, H. D. (eds), *Management Problems in Africa* (London: Macmillan).

TAVISS, I. (1970) *The Computer Impact* (Englewood Cliffs, New Jersey: Prentice-Hall).

TAYLOR, D. R. S., and OBUDHO, R. A. (1977) *The Computer and Africa*, (New York: Praeger).

THOMAS, D. BABATUNDE (1976) *Importing Technology into Africa: Foreign Investment and the Supply of Technology Innovations* (New York: Praeger).

UNITED NATIONS (1971) *The Application of Computer Technology for Development* (ST/ECA/136).

WALLACE, JOHN B. (1977) 'Computer Use in Independent Africa: Problems and Solution Statement', in Taylor, D. R. S. and Obudho, R. A. (eds), *The Computer and Africa* (New York: Praeger).

2 Data Processing: an Overview

Jan Prickett

2.1 INTRODUCTION

Data processing: the operations performed on data, usually by automatic equipment, in order to derive information or to achieve order among files.

It is important to first realize what the term 'data processing' means in the most general sense. As the above definition implies, data processing can be divided into the following steps.

1. the collecting of facts
2. the manipulating of those facts
3. the presenting of the results.

Therefore, data processing was an activity performed long before the advent of the computer age. Ancient civilisations maintained written records. Commercial records were kept on clay tablets. Collection, inventory, and distribution of items was recorded and used in decision making. Pre-electronic, mechanical devices cranked out calculations. In the early nineteenth century, 'difference' machines calculated mathematical tables; and later, modern 'adding' machines allowed mechanical arithmetic. Non-computerised electrical devices maintained records well into the twentieth century.

Data processing, as it is thought of today, is a relatively new phenomenon. It was not until the 1960s that modern electronic computers became widely popular in the business world. Today, when one refers to data processing, he is speaking of the use of computers in managing data. As mentioned in the previous chapter, the computer has become the most recent tool in the quest to turn data into information.

13

2.2   WHAT IS DATA PROCESSING?

Data processing can be summarised as the converting of data into information. 'Data' and 'information' are terms generally applied, respectively, to the preprocessing and postprocessing materials of data processing. Data is a collection of all the characters which represent values and descriptive facts operated upon during processing. Examples of data include monetary amounts, names, addresses, and groups of words which describe items. Information is the output formulated when data is manipulated and functionally organised. Examples of information include calculated numbers, lists of similar items, and plotted numeric results. To derive information from data, it must be processed. Processing is the handling and manipulation of data which changes the data into information. If one was to solve a mathematical equation, the calculations involved in arriving at a solution would represent the processing. The numeric values given to the variables would be the data. The information derived would be the answer when the calculations were complete.

2.3   DATA PROCESSING FUNCTIONS

Data processing functions are common to all types of data processing. Whether one is maintaining the inventory of a clothing store, or recording the invoices of a manufacturing company, the processing functions used are the same. Not all of the processing functions are used during any one processing task, but the pool of functions is available from which to draw as one needs. The functions can be divided into two groupings: (1) data handling functions, and (2) data manipulation functions. These groupings can be subdivided as follows:

Data handling:
1. recording
2. storage
3. retrieval
4. reporting
5. inquiry
6. communication

Data manipulation:
1. sorting
2. classification
3. selection
4. calculation
5. summarisation
6. updating

Data handling

The functions of data handling involve the management of data. The listings in this grouping specify the manner in which data can be transmitted, or moved, from one location to another;

1. *Recording*

The recording of data involves the fixation of representations which indicate real activities. Without a computer, one could record the data of a sales transaction (a real activity) by writing the details of the sale upon paper. With a computer, one could enter the details of the sales transaction into the computer by means of electronic pulses. By using either pencil and paper or computer the letters, numbers, and special characters which represent the sales transaction have been recorded. An example will help to clarify the various functions which we are considering. Consider a retail store called The Clothing Store. As clothes are purchased wholesale from various manufacturers and arrive at The Clothing Store, the purchases must be recorded. Whether one uses pencil and paper or a computer, recording is a necessary function.

2. *Storage*

Once the data has been recorded, it has to be stored for future use. All businesses and organisations have the need to place data in a safe place for future reference. The receiving records of The Clothing Store would be placed in a file with other past purchase documents. If pencil and paper had been used, the paper documents would be placed in a standard filing cabinet. If a computer had been used, the data would also be stored as an individual document with other similar documents, as a collection of magnetic images, and would also be referred to as a 'file'.

3. *Retrieval*

Retrieval is the process of recalling data from storage for referral. Retrieval causes the function of storage to be fulfilled. There would be no use in storing data if it could not be recalled. Thus, we can manually pull data from a filing cabinet, or we can use a computer to read data from a magnetic storage medium. Having retrieved the data from storage, the data exist within the computer for further processing.

4. *Reporting*

Reporting allows us to use the data which have been recorded, stored, and retrieved. The reports which are produced are formatted and manipulated in specific ways which allow the contents of files to communicate specific meaning to the users. The data of the files are processed into information, and then presented as reports. Reporting can be done manually. Papers can be retrieved from the cabinets of The Clothing Store and manually changed and formed into report documents. Computers can also perform the function of reporting. The data which is retrieved from storage can be arranged and manipulated ('Data Manipulation' is covered below) electronically. The information which results from this processing can be reported in several ways. Documents may be printed on paper as is done manually, or the information may be displayed on a monitor. The management of The Clothing Store would require inventory reports at periodic intervals. They would want to review the inventory file in order to reorder items of clothing, to chart the sales volume trends, and to check the data against store inventory counts.

5. *Inquiry*

Inquiry is the data processing function which allows one to inspect or withdraw specified data from a stored file. To inquire is to look into a file. Inquiry may be performed in order to select limited data from a single document, or to select an entire document for viewing. Manually, one could inquire into a file by physically removing a document from the filing cabinet. Electronically, a person could obtain identical data using a computer. The computer would be provided with a request using a pre-established coding system. Within a fraction of a second, the specified data would be displayed on a monitor, or begin to be printed upon paper. At The Clothing Store, data will be needed which is found within the inventory file. If this data is a very small part of the entire inventory file, inquiry would be a much better access method than printing the entire file as a report. The total item count of a piece of clothing could be obtained by using the identification number of the clothing. The computer would receive the identification number from the person using the computer, and would then search the inventory file for a matching number. When the match was made, the computer would pull the item count from the file and display the count quantity to the user of the computer. If required, all data concerning the item in question could be printed or displayed for the computer user. To perform this task manually, an employee of The Clothing Store could walk to the location of a filing cabinet and search the contents of the file for the required data. The use of a computer saves time, is more convenient, and reduces the possibility of error.

6. *Communication*

Data is not used only at the location of its physical storage. Data must often be transferred from one location to another. Sometimes, it is required to send data between locations that are separated by hundreds or thousands of kilometres. This need to transfer data from one location to another location is fulfilled by the data processing function called communication. In the past, data communication has been satisfied by the use of postal services, personal couriers, or other similar methods. Computers provide much more efficient data communication. Data stored in one computer system can be sent to another computer by means of telephone lines (and by other speed-of-light means). The computer store in our example would have the ability to check the inventory of another computer store which is at a great distance. Inventory records could be sent to the home office in seconds.

We have now reviewed the manner in which data is 'handled' in a data processing environment. For many centuries data processing has been a requirement of civilisation. Data has been recorded, stored, retrieved, reported, inquired upon, and communicated. The computer is only the most recent tool which allows these functions of data processing to be performed. As previously mentioned, there is also the need to 'manipulate' data.

Data manipulation

The functions of data manipulation involve the changing of data. The listings in this grouping specify the manner in which data can be altered, or used to create additional data. Data manipulation consists of sorting, classification, selection, calculation, summarisation, and updating. Each of these is graphically shown in figure 2.1, and is described below;

Sorting

Sorting is the act of arranging data in ascending or descending sequence. The order may be based upon either numeric or alphanumeric values. Sorting is a manipulation function which allows one to achieve control over the data as a whole. Other functions allow control over only parts of the data. Sorting is a function which is often performed as an initial step in data processing. Data must often be arranged in a specific order before it can be classified, updated, or otherwise processed. Sorting data allows one to give the data prearranged order for ease of use. Inventory files at The Clothing Store would have to be sorted before reports or displayed data could be produced. Data processing is the procedure by which order is created among files. Sorting is elementary in this ordering process.

Classification

Classification is the separation of data with similar characteristics into unique categories. This separation into groups allows one to reduce the complexity of dealing with data. Without classification, one must study large volumes of integrated data in order to reach conclusions. The massive volume of the data involved would often cause the study to be impractical or even impossible. With classification, the required data can be viewed in orderly sequence for decision-making. A purchasing manager of The Clothing Store may wish to see the total numbers of suits and coats in inventory. The decision of which suits to reorder would, if the list was unclassified, require the manager to scan the entire inventory list. If the list was first classified, the study of the inventory file would be facilitated. Classification allows more efficient use of data by separation into groups.

Selection

The data processing function which allows one to extract specific types of data from a file is called selection. Selection, like classification, makes it easier to use large volumes of data. If one needed to view only five entries in a file of ten thousand entries, the search for the five entries

Figure 2.1 Types of data manipulation

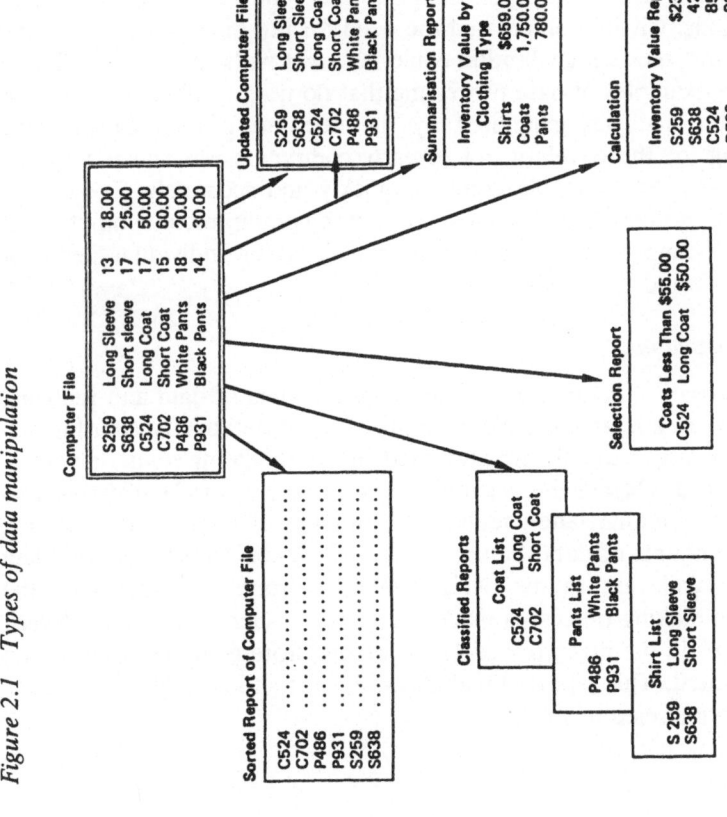

would require much time. The process of obtaining the entries would be much more efficient if the five entries could be electronically pulled (selected) from the file. These selected entries could then be displayed for the requesting person. At The Clothing Store, individual file entries could be viewed. A specific type of item could be searched for, and if found, data concerning the item would be displayed.

Calculation

Calculation is the most familiar of the data manipulation functions. Everyone is dependent upon the power and convenience of arithmetic operations. Civilisation created the need for the manipulation of numbers; now, modern civilisation could not exist without that skill. There are few examples of data processing that do not include numbers. The computer age was generated by the need to process calculations. Funding for the development of early computers was spurred by the military's need to handle numbers quickly and accurately. Today, the world of business would collapse without the omnipresent computer. At The Clothing Store, total inventory values for individual items of clothing could be calculated.

Summarisation

Summarisation involves reviewing large amounts of data and reducing that data to a relatively small quantity of representative facts or figures. Summarising is usually accomplished by accumulating numeric values, and then displaying the accumulated sums. As with classification and selection, summarisation reduces the amount of time spent reviewing larger amounts of data. Summarisation allows one to see just the data which is relevant to the decision-making process. In this way, the decision-making process is made more cost-efficient. The costs of various items in the inventory of The Clothing Store could be summarised and printed. This report would allow the correct levels of merchandise to be maintained in stock.

Updating

The last of the data manipulation functions in our list is updating. Updating is the process by which a body of data is changed to reflect current status. Data is collected and stored in order to provide information concerning a given physical reality. When the reality of a situation changes, the body of stored data which reflects that situation must also be changed. The updating function allows data to be added, deleted, or changed. Updating is obviously an indispensable feature of data processing. The number of cases where data remains unchanged is very small. The inventory of The Clothing Store will constantly be changing. Sales and the arrival of new merchandise will occur with regularity. Prices will change periodically as items become more expensive or as prices are reduced in order to increase sales.

2.4 THE DATA PROCESSING CYCLE

Those who need to process data usually need to repeat the processing activity at regular intervals of time. It is not often that a series of processing functions are established, performed once, and then permanently set aside.

The 'data processing cycle' refers to a recurring procedure by which a processing activity is performed repeatedly over an extended period of time. Common examples of processing activities are as follows:

At specified periods of time, pay cheques must be printed for employees. Names, hours worked, pay rate, and other data are used, and pay cheques are the resulting information.

Financial planning is required for an organisation or a government. Data are collected concerning the decision, statistical analysis is performed, and information is produced which allows officials to arrive at reasonable objectives.

Each processing activity must be designed by competent individuals who understand the steps by which the information is to be derived. These individuals build a cycle of functions which will reach the prescribed goal. This cycle of functions is known as a 'data processing cycle'. A particular data processing cycle is specifically designed to repeatedly accept similar data, process this data in a prescribed manner, and provide the user of the cycle with the needed information. The functions from which the data processing cycle is built are those previously described. These data handling and data manipulation functions can be divided and distributed into various aspects of the data processing cycle.

The data processing cycle can be graphically illustrated as in figure 2.2. The four aspects of the cycle are shown as rectangles. The flow of data between the aspects is illustrated by the arrows. The cycle consists

Figure 2.2   The processing cycle

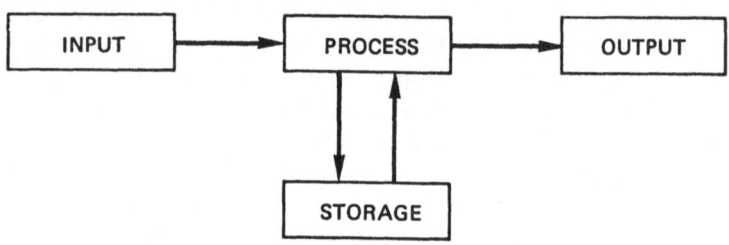

Figure 2.3   Data processing functions

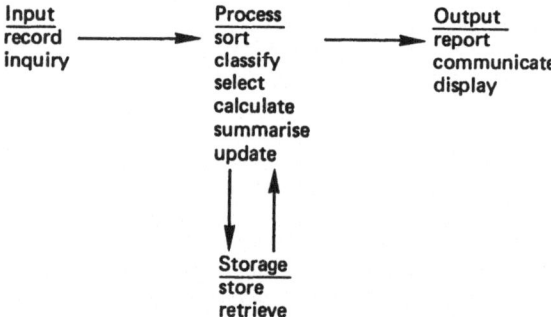

of input, processing, output, and storage. Documents containing data are collected and used as input for the cycle. This data is then operated upon in a prescribed manner (processed), and the resulting information is output. Storage is accessed by the processing aspect of the cycle. The results of processing can be sent to storage and preserved. The contents of storage can also be retrieved and used within processing. The data processing functions are used within the data processing cycle as shown in figure 2.3.

2.5   THE DATA PROCESSING SYSTEM

The data processing system is composed of all those elements which are required to implement the data processing cycle. Before the use of computers, those required elements were data, personnel, and the physical devices used by the personnel. The people of ancient civilisations used styluses to record data upon clay tablets. In this century, personnel have processed data with pencils, paper, various types of mechanical calculators, and filing cabinets. The advent of computers changed and added to the elements which compose the data processing system. Data and personnel remained integral parts of the system. The category of 'physical devices' was changed drastically.

The four aspects of the data processing cycle, as shown in figure 2.2, represent the need for physical devices within a computer data processing system. The device which accomplishes the actual processing of the data is called a processor unit (the processor unit is often referred to as the computer itself). Input is peformed by input devices such as keyboards, or card readers. Output is obtained from printers, and display screens. Storage is accomplished by computer storage media such as magnetic disks or tapes connected to the processor unit. In a computer environment, these physical devices are known as hardware.

A new element which became necessary in the data processing system was software i.e. the programs which tell the computer what to do. Hardware can not process data by itself. The pieces of hardware must be instructed how to work with one another; the processor unit must be told what functions to perform and how to perform them. This is the job of computer software. Software comprises instructions, residing in or placed into computer memory, which control the activities of the hardware.

2.6 DATA PROCESSING AND COMPUTER INFORMATION SYSTEMS

We have now looked at data processing, the cycle of data processing, and the data processing system. Emphasis has been placed upon the pure concept of data processing; without respect to time. There were occasions when it was necessary to specifically mention computers as they apply to data processing. But, the important concept to convey is that data processing is a necessary human activity. The decision of which tools to use in order to achieve data processing goals must be made by reviewing individual needs. Computers are simply the most modern of the tools at mankind's disposal.

In order to process data, collections of resources must be gathered. These collections are generically called data processing systems, or 'information systems'. When a computer is included in an information system, the system is usually referred to as a 'computer information system' (CIS). Computer information systems have obvious advantages over non-computerised information systems in that they are more convenient to use, maybe more cost-effective, faster, provide information which is more timely, and are more accurate. In order to further understand the processing of data by computer information systems, the hardware and the software which compose a CIS is explored in the following chapters.

References

ADAMS, DAVID R.; WAGNER, GERALD E.; and BOYER, TERRENCE J., *Computer Information Systems: An Introduction* (Cincinnati, Ohio: South-Western Publishing Co., 1983).

COVVEY, H. DOMINIC, and MCALISTER, NEIL, *Computer Consciousness* (Reading, Massachusetts: Addison-Wesley Publishing Company, 1980).

HAROLD, FRED G., *Introduction to Computers* (St. Paul, Minnesota: West Publishing Co., 1984).

HOPPER, GRACE, and MANDELL, STEVEN, *Understanding Computers* (St. Paul, Minnesota: West Publishing Co., 1984).

SANDERS, DONALD, *Computers Today* (New York: McGraw-Hill Inc., 1983).

SHELLY, GARY, and CASHMAN, THOMAS, *Introduction to Computers and Data Processing* (Fullerton, California: Anaheim Publishing Co., 1980).

3 Computer Hardware Considerations

Rick D. Stuart

3.1 INTRODUCTION

Hardware represents the most visible and usually the most expensive component of any data processing system. There is no facet of modern computer operations that is not in some way affected by the nature of the hardware used to support those operations, either directly or indirectly. Today, as the quality of highly specialised software for business and educational applications continues to grow, the quality of the physical devices used to adapt such software to modern problem-solving methodologies is becoming a vital consideration that cannot be underestimated in the proper designing and implementation of new data processing environments.

As the importance of the computer in the information age grows, it is vital that today's manager understands the value of hardware responsive to human needs and is aware of the interrelationships between different components making up an electronic information system. While no computer can ever be so constructed as to ideally be capable of solving every processing requirement that can develop over an extended period of time, by selecting the proper hardware the system's developer can do much to ensure that a wide range of tasks can be managed efficiently and effectively, with a minimum of financial liability. Conversely, selecting the wrong types of hardware for specific applications can adversely affect the way in which processing operations will be conducted, both in the present and the future. This being the case data processing personnel must continually strive to match the right type of hardware with specific information needs. This fundamental concern cannot be ignored without serious financial consequences in overall system performance.

This chapter aims at familiarising data processing professionals in developing third world nations with key hardware features related to equipment typically found in standard computer systems throughout the world today and with factors and considerations that influence proper hardware selection.

3.2   TERMINOLOGY

At the outset it is necessary to establish a proper understanding of what exactly is meant by the term *hardware*. When the user typically refers to a computer, in reality what one is describing is a collection of different components all working together to accomplish a given task. Such a collection is referred to as a computer *system*. The components that make up a typical system are: hardware, software, procedures, data and personnel. Hardware comprises the visible, physical devices used to carry out specific processing needs. Software refers to specific instructions written in a given language in the form of applications used by the computer to allow for user interaction and the carrying out of specific processing tasks. Procedures include instructions for personnel defining the proper conduct of routine processing operations and the proper utilisation of system equipment. Data refers to detailed specifics on transactions, business operations, financial particulars, etc. with personnel referring to the individual users interacting with the system as a whole. Together these separate and distinct elements work to accomplish specific functions involving the processing of *data* into a more manageable form commonly referred to as information. In discussing hardware the user should keep in mind that one is concerned with but one of several interrelated parts of a processing system.

Analogue and digital computer systems

Computer systems can be referred to as being either *digital* or *analogue* in nature. These two distinctions point to the different ways in which data will be represented while residing in the system. Digital computers represent the most common form of computer system in use today and represent data as a series of one's and zero's in specific patterns ('bits') stored electromagnetically within the computer's memory. Groups of these individual numeric patterns are in turn combined as 'bytes' each taking on the characteristics of a given letter, number or special symbols. Digital computers are primarily found employed in areas of business, education and industrial application. By comparison analogue computers use *measurements* rather than letters or numbers as data. These are generally provided through the use of sensitive devices employed to examine environmental surroundings, converting their findings into quantifiable terms such as temperature, weight, velocity, etc. In an analogue system numbers are represented by the magnitude (voltage) of a given electronic signal. Digital computers rely on the presence or absence of given packets of electrical current ('on-off designations') rather than actual signal magnitude to determine numerical values. Analogue computers represent specialised systems ideally suited for scientific inquiry. Whereas digital computers rely on human interaction to capture and record data to be used in processing tasks, analogue computers collect their data automatically. For the sake of simplicity, any further reference in this book to 'computers' will be taken to refer to digital computers used primarily for business applications.

Data processing networks

One special type of computer system worth noting involves the data processing network. Data communications can be thought of as the transmission of data to or from one location to another. Data is typically transmitted from one node to another in fixed length segments called 'packets'. Packets generally range in size between 1000 and 2000 bits, transmitted on a 'store and forward later' basis. Such transmission requires a data communication network. Such networks consist of a set of 'nodes'. Nodes may represent single terminals or complete computer systems connected together by one or more communication links. These links are communication pathways, typically, (but not exclusively), private or switched lines leased from a common carrier. Data communication applications include data collection, information inquiries and remote site processing.

   Given that specific needs vary from one location to another, data communication networks will necessarily vary in their final form. Nevertheless, each will typically be designed with terminals, modems, communication control units and common carrier peripherals. In actual operation such communication networks can typically be configured either as 'point-to-point' or some form of 'distributed' arrangement. In the former arrangement there exists a single communication pathway between individual nodes while in the later option there can exist more than one pathway between individual locations.

Generic and non-generic hardware

In this chapter the term *hardware* collectively refers to all physical devices utilised in a computer system. Thus hardware will now be reviewed in terms of type and function, omitting specific references to individual manufacturers. In reading this chapter, the user will come to understand not only what functions specific types of hardware perform, but also what criteria can be used to make a rational decision when choosing from among different manufacturing options. Hardware used in computer systems can be divided into two distinct categories: *generic hardware* and *non-generic hardware* . The former comprises those types of physical components every system must have present in order to complete selected processing tasks. The latter, often referred to as 'peripherals', are devices which, while not absolutely necessary in order for the system to complete basic processing tasks, are valued for the additional functionality they bring to a given system. Generic hardware in turn comprises three different types of equipment each computer system must have present in order to carry out basic processing tasks: input devices, the central processing unit and output devices. Each of these will be briefly discussed in turn below.

3.3 INPUT DEVICES

Input devices include a wide range of different equipment types all of which are fundamentally designed to facilitate the collection and transmission of data to the system's central processing unit (CPU). Input units can vary in size and versatility depending on the characteristics of the data to be entered. Card readers, for example, capture and record data through a process of translating coded series of holes punching into paper cards. More sophisticated devices such as optical character readers visually scan text or standardised forms, matching patterns detected with pre-programmed shapes identified as belonging to individual letters, numbers and symbols.

The input device most commonly encountered is the typewriter-style keyboard connected to a cathode ray tube, typically referred to as a CRT or visual display terminal VDT. All input devices can be referred to as being either 'intelligent' or 'dumb' devices based on the machine's ability to process data independent of a larger computer system given the presence of its own internal microprocessor. Dumb terminals acting as 'slaved' devices to remote systems are incapable of independent processing. Terminals can likewise be thought of as being either batch or interactive in nature. Batch terminals are used to facilitate the transmission of data to a host computer system from remote, off-site locations via communication links. These links may be either 'dedicated lines' which have a permanent connection to the host machine or may be 'dial-up lines' which handle regular telephone transmission instructions sent via a batch terminal are set to execute at a pre-determined time following their reception. Other common features input devices share include data speed, display clarity, keyboard design and physical size. *Data speed* refers to the speed with which data is transmitted from an input device to a host computer and is gauged in terms of the device's 'baud rate', a unit of measurement which represents a finite number of data 'bits' per second. A collection of bits, (typically seven or eight), are used to form a single character. Baud rates commonly range between 300 and 9600 bits per second (BPS). In cases wherein multiple users are carrying out processing tasks while jointly connected to the same computer, (what is referred to as a time-sharing system), multiple demands for computer resources can measureably degrade normal transmission and response times. The system developer must weigh factors such as maximum number of users and anticipated increases in future system demands when determining the minimum practical data speed required, relative to normal operating needs.

In the case of the video display terminal *display clarity* refers to the ease with which the individual user can work with data displayed on a phosphor screen monitor as data is entered or information received. Clarity is dependent on a number of factors which include, but are not limited to, character size and resolution, screen size and phosphor content and keyboard design. Keyboard design considers the physical layout of the input device's keypads, in particular cursor control and special function keys, as well as the physical dimensions of the keyboard. The presence of cursor control keys aid in guiding the movement of the device's cursor on the display screen without necessarily affecting text currently being displayed. Special function keys are keys which can be dedicated to addressing a specific function, the use of which replace the need for multiple instructions or keystrokes. In many cases users will define their own special functions on programmable function keys with a corresponding savings in time and effort.

VDT controversy

In recent years there has been considerable discussion concerning possible harmful effects related to prolonged use of VDTs, most notably in terms of tissue and organ damage from low level radiation attributed to these sources. While the results from numerous studies on potential hazardous affects continue to invite debate, several governments have begun to examine this question seriously for the first time. In particular the Swedish government has seen fit to require that all future governmental VDT purchases meet new, more stringent limitations for low level radiation emission and corresponding electrostatic fields. Despite this, and similar developments, there is little reason to suggest that routine utilisation of VDTs represents a noticeable health hazard to the average user working in conditions where adequate lighting and seating arrangements have been provided.

3.4   CENTRAL PROCESSING UNIT

At the heart of the computer system is the central processing unit (CPU), containing arithmetic logic and controller units, which are involved in the processing of data fed into it from one or more input devices. Arithmetic logic units are that portion of the machine where numerical operations and logical computations are performed. The control unit is that portion of the CPU where inputed instructions are decoded and operations are assigned to a portion of the arithmetic logic unit. Central processing units permit the manipulation of numeric and character-string data and most commonly allow for operations involving either fixed-point or floating-point arithmetic data representations. Fixed-point arithmetic involves binary integer arithmetic performed in the CPU's sixteen general registers. This varies from decimal arithmetic in which packed decimal representations of data are made with storage-to-storage calculations on variable length data fields. Floating-point arithmetic operations typically involve calculations with large numeric values in which the data is composed of a fraction and an exponent to express numbers that vary greatly in magnitude.

The central processing unit additionally houses the system's main core memory, often referred to as the system's main memory, in which data and information are stored. Processor memory is typically stored in a primary and secondary format. Primary, or core memory, represents the maximum amount of data and information the computer can effectively process at any given point in time. This internal limit reflects both data entered and instructions being executed. Core memory need not necessarily reflect the total amount of memory available to the user, merely the maximum amount of material in the form of programs of data sets that can be accessed at any given time. Core memory is typically presented in two forms, volatile and permanent. In the event of sudden loss of electrical power in volatile memory systems, information not as yet recorded on the system's storage disks is lost. Permanent memory systems effectively save files presently open in the event of accidental or emergency power loss.

Secondary, or auxiliary, memory reflects alternate data storage options that do not reside in the actual core of the computer's CPU. Auxiliary memory is available in numerous commercial forms and differing levels of sophistication, including, but not limited to, key-punched cards, magnetic tape, magnetic floppy or hard disks, and magnetic bubble memory. Whichever form is selected, auxiliary memory permits the storing of data and programs for future use upon demand. Computer systems, it should be noted, are not restricted to the exclusive use of one or the other types of memory presented here. Some combination of the different types is generally desirable for maximum system utility. One factor affecting CPU performance and available memory is the computer's Operating System; essentially an original program designed to permit the computer to interpret commands and determine the means by which commands will be acted upon. Different manufacturers produce different operating systems and occasionally, even under the aegis of a single manufacturer, different (and very often incompatable) operating systems will exist for different computers designed for different processing applications. Operating system programs by their very nature are both complex and memory consuming. Computer systems with increased or enhanced functionality demand a corresponding cost in the amount of memory 'overhead' demanded by the computer's larger operating system.

3.5 OUTPUT DEVICES

Output devices are the means by which processed data is displayed to the user in the form of information. Generic output devices are categorised as being either *soft copy* or *hard copy* in nature. Soft copy output devices are commonly VDTs. Input terminals can also double as an output device, permitting the user to both input data and also have acknowledgements or query responses appear on the same monitor from the CPU. In this regard the input terminal is often referred to as a dual function device due to its ability to both send data inputs and receive information in return. The term 'soft copy' refers to the way in which the data or information is displayed by scrolling one line of text at a time onto a phosphor screen. Such a display is not permanent and will be lost when the machine is shut off or another task begun.

Hard copy devices have the means of producing a lasting, 'hard', physical copy of material otherwise displayed on a terminal screen. Hard copy devices are typically printers. All hard copy printers have three main features for the prospective user's consideration: speed, character formation and type quality. In terms of speed the distinction is made between *serial* and *line* printers. Serial printers reproduce a single character of text at a time much like the common typewriter. Line printers form an entire line, typically up to either 80 or 132 characters in length, at a time. Speed is measured in CPS (Characters Per Second). Character formation refers to the actual means by which text is transferred to paper. In this printers are further characterised as either *impact* or *non-impact* devices. Impact devices require a selected key to strike an inked ribbon, thus forming the desired character. Non-impact devices such as thermal and laser printers use other means to produce the text in question.

Type quality is the fundamental factor to which all other printer considerations are subordinated. Type quality is generally categorised as either *dot matrix* or *letter quality* printers. The former category refers to text in which separate characters are composed of numerous individual dotted patterns formed from the various pinheads making up the character's key. Letter-quality printers, most notably the so-called 'daisy-wheel' printer, produce text with the clarity of type-written or professionally printed work. (The name daisy-wheel refers to the circular positioning of character blocks at the end of slender metal or plastic stalks not unlike the petals of a daisy.) Non-impact printers work without contact between the printing element and the paper. Non-impact printers can be divided into face-character and dot-character categories. Face-character non-impact printers use a xerographic process based on static electricity and photoconductivity. Dot-character non-impact printers may typically use either ink-jet or thermal processes. Ink-jet printers use electrically-charged droplets of ink shaped by minute electric fields as they are focused toward the paper. Thermal printers generate heat on styli in contact with thermochromatic paper impregnated with special chemical compounds which change colour in the pattern of a given character as the styli come in contact with the paper.

3.6 NON-GENERIC HARDWARE

Non-generic hardware, often referred to by the term 'peripherals', comprises specific devices within a computer system which, while not mandatory, nevertheless provide additional functionality and utility to the system as a whole. Non-generic devices typically fall into one of the following categories: input/output support devices, communications peripherals, and additional storage devices.

Non-generic input/output devices

Input and output support devices are commonplace to any large or multi-user computer system. Typical input/output support peripherals include hard copy console terminals, secondary line printers, graphics terminals and optical character readers. Hard copy console terminals are used whenever there is a need to capture and record a permanent record of system operations for later review. Such is typically the case whenever the system manager requires operational control of the system while excluding other users, as in the case when performing system maintenance or software installations. Console printer terminals are likewise recommended in recording the results of various systems diagnostic routines performed on a regular basis. Secondary line printers, while not providing letter quality output are, nevertheless, useful whenever physical copies of documentation are to be generated for later analysis in the shortest possible time. Computer graphics can be thought of as the design, editing, storage, retrieval and outputing of data and information in pictorial form. Computer graphics peripherals can include such input devices as optical scanners or graphics terminals to interpret data and transmit such data to the computer's memory (essentially pattern-recognition devices), and output devices such as pen plotters and graphics printers capable of producing a physical representation of the pictorial data, subject to modification by the user beforehand. Such output devices can be either two or three-dimensional in nature. Examples of the former include x – y coordinate graphs, blueprints and plots of mathematical formulae and functions. Three-dimensional representations can include cartographic and geographic displays, computer assisted design engineering models and a variety of computer animations.

Optical character readers

Optical character readers interpret data displayed in printed form on a given document, represented either as conventional bar codes or standard alphanumeric text. Optical character readers typically function in one of several standard ways: either by means of mechanical disk, photocell matrix or raster scan. The first involves covering a document with light. Between the document and a single photocell is a rapidly spinning disk covered with special slots through which 'slices' of light framing a given character are broken down for optical examination. A rapid series of character slices in a given intensity as seen by the photocell are interpreted as being identified with a particular letter or symbol. In the matrix option the character to be interpreted is projected over a matrix of numerous photocells. As scanned by the photocell, not unlike the human eye functions, if the character covers a set percentage of the photocells it is correctly 'recognised' a particular character 'value'. With a raster scan a beam from a cathode-ray tube is moved across a character in a prearranged scanning pattern in which the beam alternately moves up and down over the character. Light reflected from the beam is analysed for character recognition. Specialised optical character readers may also be used to examine forms imprinted with magnetic-ink. Applications for such devices include cheque and credit-card applications where magnetic-ink reduces the likelihood of errors in character reading due to over-printing or smudging. (Note that depending on the type of data processing tasks required optical character readers may be used either as the primary means of data input or optionally as peripherals).

Graphics terminals

Graphics terminals, (specialised VDTs designed for use in the creation and display of pictorial image-oriented data) in recent years have gained in functionality with recent advances in associated technology. In determining the utility of a given graphics terminal the following considerations should be weighed: resolution, chromaticism, terminal emulation and input/output device interfacing. Resolution, measured in individual picture elements (pixels) is the single most important quality of a graphics terminal and the larger the number of pixels that can be displayed, generally the sharper the overall graphics resolution will be. Typical graphics terminals reflect pixel ranges from a few hundred to several thousands of pixels, measured both horizontally and vertically. Chromaticism refers to the range of colours available to the user for visual presentations. While colour as a graphics attribute is not mandatory, it is very desireable. Colour graphics terminals support a range of colours drawn from a 'palette' of available color options with the average number of selections ranging between eight and sixteen. Emulation refers, in this case, to the graphics terminals ability to display both text and graphics and to duplicate the standard functionality of a given type of VDT used with a computer system. Users are warned that manufacturer claims of emulation ability may in fact refer to only partial functionality at best. The ability to interface graphics terminals with other non-generic devices such as pen plotters and graphics-oriented printers is a final factor that will influence potential terminal selection.

Taken as a whole graphics terminals add an expanded dismension to the normal means by which data and information can be disseminated and should be given due consideration in any planned system configuration.

Non-generic communications devices

Non-generic communications devices are typically found in computer systems supporting a communications network. One example of communications peripherals has already been mentioned: the modem. Other representative examples of different 'levels' of communication peripherals include multiplexors and front-end processors. Short for modulator – demodulator, these devices are used to facilitate data transmission or reception along various voice-grade common-carrier communication lines from one node to another. At the data origin point a modem is used to modulate the signal with frequencies ranging between 300 and 3000 Hz, allowing for transmission to a pre-selected reception point where a second modem is used in turn to de-modulate the incoming signal and return it to its original digital form. Modems can be either synchronous or asynchronous in nature. Synchronous modems transmit data at a fixed baud rate with receiving modems 'synchronised' at the same rate of speed. Asynchronous modems can operate at varying speeds as may be required.

Multiplexors are peripheral devices designed to aid in data transmission by allowing for the transmission of several low-speed data streams over a single, higher-speed communication line, thus reducing associated transmission costs and reducing the possibility of errors occurring in the actual transmission process. Multiplexed data signals are particularly useful whenever independent data channels are required between two or more nodes, or whenever various data links are running parallel to each other over great distances.

Front-end processors, typically found in larger computer systems, are small digital computers programmed to take over the communications control functions of the 'host' central processor, thus permitting the main CPU to continue performing its primary data processing functions while the front-end processor handles all of the tasks associated with data transmission and reception. Such a device is particularly useful in a situation where a large volume of communications operations would otherwise degrade standard system operations or where communications efficiency can be maximised by a division of control responsibility.

Common non-generic storage options

Non-generic storage devices take advantage of both tape and disk technologies. Tape drive units aid in facilitating system backup and recovery procedures wherein important data and information files can be stored/retrieved with a minimal amount of difficulty. Tape drives likewise allow for the off-loading of material and the importation of material from one site to another. One of the most common mass storage devices is the disk storage unit consisting of a collection of rigid disks, the surfaces of which are coated to allow for magnetic storage of data, and a disk controller. Common disk packs can permit the storage of up to several million bytes worth of data at a time. Disk storage units vary depending on whether the controller's read/write heads (by which data is read or is stored onto the disks) are fixed or movable and whether the disk pack itself is fixed or removable. The latter option permits greater hardware flexibility, given the ability to interchange disk packs (and associated files) at will, the safe storage of important packs as needed, and the copying of complete disk packs, given the presence of more than one storage unit.

Disk storage units will also vary in functionality based on the time required to complete actual data transfer to and from disks to CPU primary memory. This access time (measured in milliseconds) will be a function of three individual measurements: access motion time, disk rotational delay and data movement time interval. Access motion time is that interval required to position read/write heads over the disk. Rotational delay measures the amount of time needed for the corresponding data to revolve underneath the read/write heads. Data movement time refers to the time needed for the data to be actually transferred from the disk to the memory once it has been read by the read/write heads.

Other non-generic storage options

In addition to hard disk packs or magnetic tape as storage options floppy drive and magnetic drum units may also be utilised as valid hardware options. Floppy disk units read/write data to/from CPU memory similar in nature to their hard disk counterparts. Floppy disk storage as a hardware option have the advantages of eliminating bulky hard controller units where space is at a premium and greater ease of disk (file) duplication. The major drawback to the use of floppy disks is the small amount of memory space available in comparison to hard disk options. One final storage option to be considered here is the magnetic drum on which data is recorded along its cylindrical surfaces. In addition to a smaller size, magnetic drum storage has the added advantage of eliminating access motion delays found in hard disk counterparts. While magnetic drums as common storage media have been largely replaced by other storage alternatives, they can still be considered a valid option in many cases and should not be overlooked out of hand.

3.7 SYSTEM HARDWARE SELECTION

Given the above overview of different types of generic and non-generic hardware, it remains to identify what factors influence the selection of individual hardware components and what considerations should be involved in the design of an efficient computer system. In attempting to select the proper hardware components for a given computer system it is necessary first to determine the exact nature of the system to be employed.

While a computer system can be characterised as being either digital or analogue in design, in terms of actual functional application the digital computer system, in its final form, can be one of three standard configurations: an operational system, a managerial information system or a decision support system. An operational system is a computer system designed to carry out routine data processing functions at the lowest level of day-to-day operations. Managerial information systems, in addition to processing daily data operations also create information for different managerial levels within a given firm. Decision support systems are computer systems designed to facilitate upper-level management decision-making through the use of application software and procedures developed to access data contained in pre-defined databases as well as aiding in strategic planning through the incorporation of various modelling techniques.

Having identified the particular level of computer system required and the corresponding type(s) of information to be processed, it remains to deal with several specific questions to be addressed as part of the actual hardware selection process:

1. What are my system requirements?
2. What type of environmental controls are needed for the system?
3. What type of system maintenance will be required?
4. What standards will be used to determine system reliability?
5. What criteria determine system versatility?
6. What factors influence hardware safety?

Each of these considerations is briefly examined below. Note that in many cases, while it is possible to determine a reasonably accurate model of projected hardware configurations based solely on available information provided by manufacturer or vendor service, in others estimates of specific selection considerations can best be made only through examinations of functional hardware already in place at given sites. Final evaluations of hardware for selection purposes should, practically speaking, include both types of estimations.

Defining system requirements

At the start of any hardware selection process it is essential that a proper understanding of overall system requirements be shared by those needed to manage and operate the system on a full-time basis. This is necessary given that different types of computer systems will produce different types of information. Information produced by specific computer systems will be either historical, current or future-oriented, depending on existing business cycles, and will tend to be more generalised with each level of managerial organization.

With this in mind it becomes imperative to properly identify both immediate processing needs as well as making a valid estimation of future needs over a projected period of time, anticipating increased user demands once system installation has been completed. Moreover, in attempting to estimate costs associated with the acquisition of new computer hardware system designers and project managers should likewise calculate the long-term cost of any computer system not only in terms of immediate generic hardware requirements but likewise in terms of projected peripherals and other system enhancements as may be required later. Lastly, in defining system requirements it is likewise essential that due consideration be given to responses solicited from personnel who will be expected to work directly with the hardware employed.

Hardware environment and safety

If a computer system is being installed for the first time attention should be directed towards environmental factors influencing hardware operation. If necessary projected costs should allow for a basic remodelling or even new construction of facilities where the hardware will be housed. In an ideal environment proper air conditioning, circulation and humidity controls are essential as well as other climate control devices needed in unusually hot or cold temperature zones. Non-static tile floors are also recommended to avoid unnecessary static electricity build ups. All hardware should likewise be safely positioned away from exposed heating and water pipes. Air filtration systems should be examined to ensure proper working order. Use of fire-resistant building materials in any new construction or renovations is highly recommended. Strict procedures should likewise be enforced concerning smoking or the introduction of consumables within a hardware confinement area and, with an eye towards proper security, care should be taken to avoid positioning vital equipment near easily accessible windows or doorways through which vandals could readily enter.

The protection of hardware against the threat of damage is a consideration that cannot be minimised in planning the design of any computer system. Considerations of hardware security, (like that of data security), are needed to reduce the potential risk of loss to major assets due to unforeseen circumstances, both man-made and natural in origin. While the types of security measures implemented for a given system will vary dependent on the types of hardware (and data) being used at a given location, some basic considerations can be seen here as common to every hardware configuration. (To what degree these are actually implemented will depend, however, largely on external design limitations and budgetary constraints).

Provision should be made for backup power sources used to provide electrical power under various emergency conditions. Such devices should be capable of powering all generic hardware components, temperature regulation, air conditioning and environmental control systems, any communications peripherals present and such on-site security devices as may be in place. Likewise the utilisation of fire detection and containment devices such as smoke and heat sensing devices, portable extinguishers and sprinkler systems combined with adequate training for system's personnel is mandatory. Equally important, though less visible, is the need for established emergency control procedures for personnel. Adequate provision of clearly-worded and understood policies concerning safety measures such as emergency hardware shutdown procedures, priority removal of memory media (disk packs, etc). cannot be under-rated. Likewise provision should be taken to establish disaster-recovery procedures whereby restoration of crippled systems can be completed with minimal delay. Given the probability of a clearly perceived threat to the system it may be adviseable in terms of system redundancy to duplicate generic system components at a secondary location under conditions of maximum security.

Hardware maintenance

Even the most sophisticated and expensive computer hardware designed by a prestigious manufacturer can malfunction. A frequent source of hardware faults in a given system will lie with the various input/output devices. Mechanical components in these devices are subject to a higher incidence of failure due to excessive use. Also common is a failure of the system's memory media (either primary or auxiliary) through exposure to dust or dirt. In terms of overall hardware maintenance, due to the complexity of modern computer equipment in general few users will have the needed technical or mechanical skills necessary to maintain their own system but will likely choose instead to enter into a maintenance agreement with the system's manufacturer throughout the lifetime of the system. Sometimes more than one maintenance agreement will be required given the presence of different manufacturers' hardware in the same system. The intrinsic value of purchasing such 'foreign' component(s) should be evaluated against such added expenses. While the 'overhead' costs that are associated with such contracts over an extended period of time can be excessive, such costs must be weighed against the alternative costs associated with staffing the hardware site with trained personnel and on-going inventories of spare parts for both generic and non-generic hardware. Given that the latter option is not considered a viable one, the issue of manufacturer or vendor support becomes critical. Manufacturer's support should extend beyond routine system inspections on a periodic basis. The real test of support personnel lies in emergency situations where the threat of lost data or the need for speedy operation restoration is imperative.

Hardware reliability

In assessing system hardware reliability two specific factors must be taken into consideration: equipment availability and maintainability. The term 'availability' here refers to overall system functionality. Availability also refers to the probability that a given system components will remain operative over a given period of time. Availability typically is expressed mathematically as the value of the total anticipated amount of functional time anticipated (in days, hours, etc) in a given time period divided by the sum of the total amount of time the component has previously been inoperative in a similar period, plus the total amount of anticipated operational time.

Maintainability is the average amount of time required to repair a given hardware failure from the point at which a malfunction is detected to the point at which the device is again fully operational. Other factors influencing overall hardware reliability are redundancy, fault tolerance and residual value. A computer system is not redundant if it contains only generic hardware or, alternatively only the minimal amount of non-generic hardware required to carry out important processing needs on a regular basis. Hardware redundancy, e.g. the presence of added hardware components to duplicate specific functions, can be considered a legitimate system design feature, if, and only if, such redundancy provides some positive benefit to the system as a whole. One example might be the presence of numerous console devices allowing system access from different locations. The mere presence of additional devices duplicating selected system features does not, in itself, create a beneficial arrangement unless there is a very high probability of hardware malfunctions over a given period of time.

Fault tolerance refers here to the ability of the computer system as a whole to continue performing processing operations in the presence of a hardware malfunction. Systems in which redundancy is kept to a minimum will have little inherent error tolerance. The breakdown of a single piece of equipment could temporarily halt normal processing routines until replacement or repair is implemented. Fault tolerance can also imply internal backup systems as part of a given piece of hardware (such as emergency power supplies) which take over internal functions in the event of a malfunction. In either case the cost of factoring in high levels of error tolerance must be weighed against the potential costs involved in the accidental loss of data or time through a serious system malfunction.

The residual value of any piece of computer equipment must be considered against the actual long-term maintenance costs needed to keep such equipment functional over a given period of time. With respect to the actual replacement of component elements over time, larger institutions will more than likely consider the outright resale and replacement of hardware at periodical intervals in order to retain higher asset levels. Medium and smaller sized institutions will be more apt to retain depreciated hardware, eventually passing on such equipment to other users with fewer processing demands as time goes on. System hardware in general can be rated for reliability based on manufacturer's estimates of the normal average functioning period between two hardware malfunctions, what is known as the equipment's (or overall system's) *mean time*. Using such estimates, the ability to gauge potential effectiveness of one or more system components allows the system's manager increased flexibility in scheduling processing activities and projects. Knowing with a reasonable degree of certainty in advance when specific pieces of hardware will require major maintenance gives the administrator the opportunity to implement alternative processing options at his disposal, or to make provision for such options in advance without disrupting normal processing cycles.

System versatility

Measures of overall hardware versatility can include considerations of program portability, data retrieval through the implementation of backup and recovery policies, connectivity, and the ease with which system upgrades or enhancements can be conducted. Connectivity often involves the use of microcomputers in a communications mode, operating as the mechanism whereby selected communications software permits the transfer of files to/from larger host systems. Program portability refers to the ease with which program instructions written in a given language can be duplicated and run on another machine of different type with similar results. Programs written in assembler, for example, will necessarily be linked to a particular system's architecture and thus lack 'portability' while programs written in high-level languages increase the probability of program replication with minimal inconvenience. For this reason it is often desirable to have a system capable of supporting a minimum of two languages, one of which is a high-level language option. Care should be taken to back up sensitive or otherwise important files on a regular basis. Often a complete copy of all material currently stored in memory should be made. This can be facilitated through the availability of tape drive peripherals or additional memory units such as secondary hard disk or system floppy disk mediums. Multiple copies are often the rule, with the 'child-parent-grandparent' approach allowing maximum protection against unforseen data loss. Connectivity refers to the ability of computer systems to permit the transfer of data files from one system to another as well as general access to different system functions. A final consideration reflecting on hardware versatility is the ease with which hardware enhancements can be added to existing hardware configurations with a minimal amount of difficulty as well as overall system expansion and upgrading with an eye towards maintaining compatibility with counterpart systems at different locations. This in turn reflects on the degree of manufacturer or vendor support available, constraints imposed by existing hardware options (or lack thereof) with respect to individual manufacturers and internal hardware architecture.

Other hardware considerations

One factor which will inevitably reflect on a computer system's performance as a whole is the determination of that system's over all size, based in large part on CPU capacity and performance ratings. Regarding computers many users have the understandable misconception that bigger is always better. In many cases, however, this assumption is not always true. In determining the proper processor size and capability, (and indirectly the shape of the remaining hardware configuration as a whole), the primary consideration should remain the amount and complexity of processing tasks the hardware will be expected to deal with under routine conditions. While physical space needed to house generic equipment can be a consideration, especially when local conditions require special environmental controls for hardware safety, a more important consideration is an accurate estimate of the normal operating demands once the equipment has been installed. Related to this issue are questions of processor speed and memory. How quickly the central processor is capable of responding to processing instructions depends on related factors known as the system's *operating mean*. This term refers to a measurement of the processor's ability adequately to respond to user demands with allowances for reasonable interval's between user inquiry and system response. The operating mean is dependent upon the amount of data being manipulated, the number of users competing for access to the system at the same time and whether the CPU's operating system is multi-tasking in nature. (Multi-tasking refers to a function of the operating system which permits a single user to instruct the system to run more than one set of individual instructions/programs at a given time. This is particularly useful whenever the user needs to examine the results from more than one operation before deciding on a further course of action regarding a different software application). Processor performance and over-all system utility can similarly be affected by the amount of primary memory taken up by the computer's operating system instructions.

Care should be taken in the initial planning stages to allow for possible upgrades or enhancements of a planned operating system which will require additional memory space with succeeding versions. Failure to plan adequately in this regard may result in the need for a drastic increase in primary memory space in order to accommodate a larger operating system at a period when such expenditures are impossible. In such instances the individual users are often left with an operating system that has already been superseded by a higher version and is rapidly becoming obsolete as software manufacturer's begin designing applications solely for the more advanced operating system version(s).

3.8 FUTURE PROJECTIONS

Given the time interval inherent in the development and actual marketing of various manufacturer's hardware, it appears reasonable to assume that the majority of the hardware configurations to be employed in business and research applications throughout the late 1980s – 90s will be the same as those introduced in the late 1970s and early 1980s. The major factors that may alter this state of affairs are the possibility of unexpected breakthroughs in the areas of memory type and size, data access speeds, and the overall price of non-generic hardware. Recent developments can suggest, however, some speculations on future hardware options. For example, recent advances in very large-scale circuit integration and semiconductor materials have lead to the development of micro-sensors that accurately simulate the functions of human sight and hearing which in turn may lead to unexpected advances in artificial intelligence applications. Given such devices will provide real-time measurements of environmental conditions, these devices can be incorporated into sophisticated system microchips allowing for enhanced speed and system efficiency with a corresponding decrease in overall system costs. Similar efforts may eventually make practical voice-recognition terminals and voice-activated peripherals as generic hardware options.

In terms of memory, new alternatives including magnetic bubble memory and even organic-based memory systems are being explored and one recent innovation, the compact-disk, read-only memory employing laser light in place of standard mechanical read/write heads, offers some encouragement for users requiring massive amounts of memory capacity within minimal amounts of space. Coupled with similar advances in the development of increasingly powerful microprocessor chips, such lines of research and development may ultimately combine to produce hardware with operational characteristics unheard of within a relatively short period of time.

3.9 SUMMARY

The proper selection of computer hardware must begin with an adequate understanding of the different types of computer equipment commonly employed for various processing tasks and their relation to each other. Hardware acquisition is a dynamic process. In the selection of hardware the system designer is determining the guidelines and constraints by which processing operations will be conducted for the forseeable future. The actual process does not terminate, however, with the completed installation of the final generic device. Given sufficient planning initially, a properly designed system can continue to evolve to meet growing demands from a wide range of sources. The selection of computer hardware represents a commitment to a future course of action. Through such selections, either individually or collectively, the system manager effectively determines the way in which processing operations will be conducted for a considerable period of time to come. Once a given course of action, represented by a specific hardware configuration, has been installed, diverting from the policies and procedures that inevitably follow hardware installation can only be altered or abandoned at a considerable cost in both time and money. Therefore no piece of computer hardware should ever be purchased solely on the basis of manufacturer's reputation, but only with proper regard to the means by which the selected hardware fulfills a well-defined user need and careful evaluation to ensure the equipment brings to an existing system some tangible benefit.

References

Books

BECKER, J. and R. M. HAYES *Information Storage And Retrieval – Tools Elements, Theories* (New York: John Wiley, 1963).

BURCH, JOHN G., FELIX R. STRATER and GARY GRUDNITSKI *Information Systems: Theory and Practice* (New York: John Wiley, 1979).

DRUMMOND, M. E. *Evaluation and Measurement Techniques For Digital Computer Systems* (Englewood Cliffs, New Jersey: Prentice-Hall, 1973).

ELIASON, ALAN and KENT D. KITTS. *Business Computer Systems And Applications* (Chicago: Science Research Associates, 1979).

FOSTER, CLAXTON C. *Computer Architecture* (New York: Van Nostrand Reinhold, 1970).

IBM System/360 Disk Operating System Data Management Concepts (Order Number GC 24-3427-6) (White Plains, New Jersey: IBM Corporation Technical Publications Department, October, 1970).

KROENKE, DAVID M. *Business Computer Systems: An Introduction* (Santa Cruz, California: Mitchell Publishing, Inc., 1981).

LANGEFORS, B. and B. SUNDGREN. *Information Systems Architecture.* (New York: Petrocelli-Charter, 1975).

MEADOWS, A. J., M. GORDON and A. SINGLETON. *The Random House Dictionary of New Information Technology* (New York: Vintage Books, 1982).

RALSTON, ANTHONY and CHESTER L. MEEK. *Encyclopedia of Computer Science* (New York: Van Nostrand Reinhold Company, 1976).

RAO, GUTHIKONDA V. *Microprocessors And Microcomputer Systems* (Second Edition) (New York: Van Nostrand Reinhold Company, 1982).

SIPPI, CHARLES J. *Microcomputer Dictionary* (Second Edition). Indianapolis, Indiana: Howard W. Sams and Co., Inc., 1981).

THIERAUF, ROBERT J. *Distributed Processing Systems* (Englewood Cliffs, New Jersey: Prentice-Hall, 1978).
VAX Systems Option Catalog April – June 1986 (Maynard, Massachusetts: Digital Equipment Corporation, 1986).
WALSH, MYLES E. *Understanding Computers: What Managers And Users Need To Know* (New York: John Wiley and Sons, Inc., 1981).

Articles

BHUSHAN, A. K. 'Guidelines For Microcomputer Selection', *Computer Design*, April 1971, pp. 43–57.
MORIZT, FREDERICK G. 'Conventional Magnetic Tape Equipment' *Modern Data*, Vol. 8, No. 3, March, 1975, pp. 51–55.
NIELSEN, N. R. 'Flexible Pricing: An Approach to the Allocation of Computer Resources', *Proceedings of the Spring Joint Computer Conference, 1968*, pp. 521–531.
NOE, J. D. 'Acquiring and Using a Hardware Monitor', *Datamation*, April, 1974, pp. 89–95.
'Printers and Plotters'. *Computer Decisions*, Vol. 10, No. 8, August, 1978, pp. 60–63.
SAGE, S. M. 'Information Systems: A Brief Look Into History', *Datamation*, November, 1968, pp. 63–69.

4 Computer Software Concepts

Sudesh Duggal

4.1 INTRODUCTION

The term computer used in this chapter will be in the general sense of business computer systems. The meaning of a computer system will be explained first, then the system components will be described. Finally, one of the system components, namely software, will be discussed in detail.

A system is defined as an organised collection of components such as, equipment, skills, techniques, and information, that interact to accomplish specified management objectives. A computer system is a collection of such components, the computer being one of them, that interact to accomplish specified management objectives. Thus a computer system is not just a computer, as is often mistakenly assumed by most people, rather it is one of the components of the complete computer system.

The common misconception among management personnel is that the installation of a computer will bring an end to most of their managerial problems. But actually, it is not true, because the computer is only one of the components of a computer system, and its acquisition will create the need of other components of the computer system. This will require a considerable amount of extra expense for the working and maintenance, other than the cost of a computer.

4.2 THE COMPONENTS OF A COMPUTER SYSTEM

The five components of a computer system are hardware, software, data, procedures and personnel. Each component of the computer system is required to meet the needs of business, and if any one of these components is missing, the needs cannot be met.

Data, procedures, and personnel components have been discussed in Chapter 2, whereas the computer hardware component in Chapter 3. Computer software component is the subject of this chapter, and is given below.

4.3   COMPUTER SOFTWARE AND ITS CATEGORIES

The set of all the programs and routines that controls and operates the computer hardware is termed computer software.

Since the introduction of the computer, there have been dramatic changes in hardware, but the software development has not kept pace with hardware advances. During the last two decades the price/performance ratio of computer hardware has improved by a factor of more than a million, whereas in spite of all the improvements in software developments, the productivity of programmers have not increased by more than two or three times, over the same period. Also, the great advances in the computer hardware have exceeded the ability of ordinary data processing personnel or management. Thus in order to utilise these new capabilities, new trained personnel are needed, who are costly, and are not easily available.

Due to these reasons the development of good software is and will continue to be a slower, more expensive and time-consuming process than the hardware development. But despite all of this, there have been tremendous improvements in the development of computer software in the recent years.

The two major categories of software used in business are: Applications Software and System Software. Applications Software is oriented toward the needs of the user, and directs the computer in performing specific user-related data processing tasks. It can be purchased from the vendor of the computer or a software company or developed in-house. System software, on the other hand, controls the computer, and is designed to facilitate the use of hardware and to help the computer system operate efficiently, is usually provided by the computer manufacturer.

Application software

Application software performs specific data processing or computational tasks to solve an organisations information needs. It forms a link between a computer and its users, the people who need data processing services. In a typical business organisation, there may be a number of application programs. We can group them into two different categories.

Cross-industry software

The set of programs that perform tasks which are common to several business organisations, or user groups falls in this category. This category includes programs for applications such as Payroll, Accounts Receivable, Accounts Payable, Inventory Control, General Ledger, and Statistical Analysis.

In the past, however, much time and money has been spent by many organisations in the preparation of these programs, when they have been previously developed by other organisations. Recognizing the wastefulness of such duplication of effort, independent software firms and equipment manufacturers have developed generalised application packages, also known as packaged programs, for this category of applications.

Application software of this category is usually purchased from outside sources such as computer vendors or independent software suppliers.

Industry-specific software

The set of programs that performs tasks which are unique to a particular business organisation, or user group are in this category. The programs for such applications include mortgage loan accounting for banks, and claim management for insurance companies. The programs in this category may be developed within the organisation, by a staff of professional programmers or may be purchased from software firms.

These days, the trend is that more business organisations are purchasing application packages than are hiring professional programming staff to develop them. Some of the main reasons are that:

1. the purchasing cost of the application packages is much lower than in-house development;
2. the application packages can be implemented in much less time than the in-house produced programs;
3. the application packaged programs are generally much more reliable than in-house produced programs; and finally
4. the application packaged programs are generally more efficient than in-house developed programs.

System software

System software includes programs that affect the operation of computer hardware. They are designed to facilitate the use of computer hardware and to help the computer system run effectively and efficiently. The main function of the system software is to direct the operation of the computer, rather than the processing of data and delivery of information.

4.4 OPERATING SYSTEMS

In early computer systems, human operators had to perform initial start-up procedures and housekeeping procedures for each program to be executed on the computer system. The start-up procedures included loading data-input devices with cards and tapes, setting switches on the computer console, starting the processing of a program, preparing and unloading the output devices. The housekeeping procedures included functions, such as clearing the central processor storage locations between programs, and loading the next program and data into main storage. After the completion of each program, housekeeping and start-up procedures were repeated and this process continued throughout the day.

While the development of hardware increased the processing speed of the central processing unit, the speed of human operators remained constant. To improve the efficiency of computers, operating systems were implemented in the 1960s.

An operating system is a collection of programs used by the computer system to manage its own operations. Thus, instead of performing start-up procedures for each job, the operator only need to start-up the operating system and from there on it will have the responsibility for all the jobs to be run. This improved communication between the operator and the computer made the computer more productive, since the set-up time was reduced.

Operating systems are purchased from individual computer manufacturers and vary in size, complexity, and ability to support processing activities. The same manufacturer may offer many types of operational software, often making recommendations on which software is suited to a particular user's need.

The nucleus of the operating system is usually supplied by the vendor at no extra cost, whereas the software to provide additional features, such as a Management Information System or Database, is usually purchased or leased.

The American National Standard Institute (ANSI) defines the operating system as, 'software which controls the execution of the computer programs and which may provide scheduling, debugging, input/output controls, accounting, compilation, storage assignment, data management, and related services.'

Basically, an operating system is divided into three categories, control programs, processing programs, and data management programs.

Control programs

This part of the operating system provides automatic allocation of the computer resources to the jobs being run on the computer. These programs reduce the need for operator intervention, thus providing an orderly and efficient flow of jobs. The basic functions performed by the control programs are job management and resource management.

The job management programs are primarily responsible for the complete management of the computer system. Their functions include interpretation of the control statements, scheduling jobs for execution, handling the initiation and termination of the jobs, and providing communication between computer and operator. The resource management program mainly allocates the resources of the computer system to the programs being executed.

These two sets of programs, the job management programs and the resource management programs reside in the internal memory of the computer system during the time of its operation. These are also called supervisor programs.

Still another set of control programs which work very closely with the supervisor programs are job control programs. Their function is to provide continuity between jobs on the computer system.

Processing programs

The processing programs consist of language processors and service programs.

In the early 1950s, programs were written in the basic language of the computer, called machine language. It was tedious, time consuming, and inconvenient to program a computer using the machine language. Symbolic languages were introduced to ease the burden of the programmers. The first in this category is assembler language, a language very closely related to the machine language, in which each machine instruction is represented by a symbolic instruction. These are termed low-level languages.

With the introduction of the symbolic languages, programming became a little less tedious, but still was quite difficult and inconvenient. Since symbolic languages are closely related to the machine, a good knowledge of the internal characteristics of the computer is required to program in this language. To ease the problem further, programming languages were developed in which the program statements are not closely related to the internal characteristics of the computer. These languages are called high-level languages. These languages are less machine-dependent than the assembler languages, and are widely used by people, because the detailed knowledge of computers is not required or needed. Language processors or language translators interpret or compile these high-level programming language codes into machine language. These translator programs are called compilers, whereas these programming languages are called compiled languages.

Service programs perform common processing tasks, which are required by programmers and operations personnel. The major categories of the service programs are linkage editor, library programs, and utility programs.

The purpose of the linkage editor is to transform the object programs generated from the language translators into load modules which are ready for execution on the computer system. The translated application program, called an object program, is not yet in a form which can be loaded into the main computer storage for execution.

The linkage editor programs include the library programs and the data management routines needed in the application programs and divide the whole object program into load modules. In addition, the task of the linkage editor is, to link the load module from the system residence device to main storage by assigning appropriate main storage addresses. After this the load modules are ready for execution.

The set of programs that are frequently used in application programs are called library programs. These are user-written or manufacturer-supplied, stored in the computer's auxiliary storage, and are called into main memory when needed by the application programs. They are linked together with application programs to perform specific tasks, and thus eliminate the need for writing them every time in the application programs. A librarian program manages the storage and use of the library programs by maintaining a directory of programs in the system library.

Service programs also include a set of utility programs which are used to transfer data from tape to tape, tape to disk, or tape to printer. The sort/merge programs, for example, are used to sort records into sequence to facilitate updating of files. After sorting, several files can be merged to form a single updated file.

Data management programs

Data management programs, typically provided by the vendor, help the user in the organisation of data stored in external computer files. The main function of these programs is to regulate the placement of data in files and to simplify the retrieval of the data stored in files. They also facilitate input and output error checking and recovery. The data management programs relieve the programmer of tedious coding of detailed instructions required to perform functions such as index maintenance, blocking and deblocking, and space allocation for files. File management programs, a subset of data management programs, simplify the planning and control procedures used to organise the storage and retrieval of data in files. Data base management programs, an extension to Data management programs, are designed to integrate sets of data contained in different computer files.

4.5 TYPES OF OPERATING SYSTEMS

Input/output control systems (IOCS) were introduced in the early 1960s. IOCS are stored in an online library and I/O control initiates, executes, monitors, and controls the transfer of data into and out of the computer.

The I/O controls software and eliminates most of the details of handling input/output operations in application software, thus making the coding easier and uniform. Also the handling of data stored on direct access devices, auxiliary storage devices which provide immediate access to individual records without sequential search, is simpler due to the availability of the control routines.

Different access methods are supported by different operating systems. Some systems require the use of a special language called

JOB CONTROL LANGUAGE (JCL), which tells the system where the data is to be stored or from where it can be retrieved.

The use of JCL also provides flexibility and provides a means of communication between the computer and the operator. Other systems support a type of dynamic storage allocation in which the programmer is not even aware of where the data is to be stored on the direct access storage device. There are four basic types of operating systems:

1. Batch Processing
2. Multiprogramming
3. Timesharing
4. Real Time

Batch processing

In a batch processing environment, jobs are stacked or stored in a sequence on an external storage device, usually a magnetic disk or tape. By the use of JCL, jobs are brought into the internal storage, one at a time, and are executed in sequence.

Job management programs determine that all the steps associated with a job are in order. Input/output control programs coordinate transfer of data to and from the central processing unit and to and from I/O devices.

The operating system of a computer allows input, data storage, data processing, data output, and data communications to take place without human intervention.

Multiprogramming

Most of the small computer systems initially start with an operating system that handles only batch processing and then add additional software that supports multiprogramming or timesharing.

The speed at which a computer performs calculations is extremely fast as compared to the speed at which even the fastest input/output devices operate. To compensate this imbalance of speed and to increase the productivity of the computer, a process called multiprogramming is used.

A multiprogramming system permits the concurrent execution of two or more programs simultaneously residing in the internal memory of a computer. It increases the computer's productivity by using

more efficiently the computational ability. While input/output operations of one program are being handled, the computational part of
the central processing unit is idle and can handle some mathematical
or logical operations of another program at the same time. Only one
instruction can be executed at a time. Since input/output activity
usually takes longer than the mathematical or logical operation, a
second program can be executing while the first program waits for
input/output to be read into memory or for output to be sent to an
output device.

Timesharing

The fast speeds of today's processors and the rapid data transfer rates
of direct access storage devices makes it possible for many users to
interact with the same system simultaneously. The speed at which the
system components operate, allows the system to switch from one
user to another, doing all or part of each program until all work is
completed. The speed may be so great that each user has the
impression of being the only one using the system.

This type of operation, whereby a computer system automatically
distributes its processing time among several users simultaneously, is
termed timesharing. In other words timesharing is the simultaneous
utilisation of a computer system by many users, and the real purpose
of it is to economise by sharing computer costs.

In timesharing, the operating system assigns a period of time called
a time slice – say, a fraction of a second – to each user. The operating
system maintains a queue of all the users of the system at a particular
time, and lets each user take his or her turn and use the Central
Processing Unit for its time slice, and when this time period runs out,
control goes to the next user. Whenever a user's program makes an
input/output request, then the user loses the rest of its time or time
slice and continue to lose their turn until the request is satisfied.

From the computers point of view, timesharing is much like multiprogramming. So what is the difference between the two?

Multiprogramming is basically used in a batch processing environment, and users do not interact directly with their programs. The
central processing unit transfer its control to another program only
when the program in control of the central processing unit issues an
input/output operation request.

Timesharing, on the other hand, is used in an on-line environment
and the users interact directly with their programs. The program's

response to the user's request should be immediate, and it should seem to the user that he has the entire computer to himself, but the fact is that he is actually sharing it with many other users. Every user gets a turn in sequence for a period of time slice unless the user's program is waiting for input/output operations to be satisfied.

Real time

A real time system is one in which data is received and processed and the users receive the results in a time fast enough to influence the ongoing transaction. The concept of real time is closely related to immediacy and requires a very fast system response time, which is the interval of time between completion of input and start of output from a computer system.

In actual operation, real time is a matter of degree, depending upon the application at hand. In an airline reservation system, response time of a few seconds may be acceptable, but in a computer-controlled military defence system, response time of a microsecond may be required.

Real time systems have the same general characteristics as time sharing systems, since many users can simultaneously have access to the computer by using terminals. However, in a real time system often one program serves all users, while in time sharing systems each user uses his or her own program.

4.6 SUMMARY

The declining cost of computer hardware has increased the computer purchasing power of business, which in turn has escalated the demand for computer software. This increase in demand for software, has resulted in the creation of large numbers of software and consulting firms. These firms usually specialise in either system software or application software, which are often sold as packaged software.

These software packages cost less, as compared to in-house developed software, can be implemented in shorter period of time, are more reliable, and are more efficient. These days, some software and consulting firms are developing customised software packages as well, on contract basis and are even providing ongoing maintenance for their software to the customers. Due to this, more and more small businesses and first users are purchasing the packaged software.

The decreasing cost of computer hardware has also resulted in an overwhelming increase in the number of computer users in the countries of the third world. Being first-time users and short of trained personnel, the development of system and application software is a major problem for them. The availability of packaged software is a blessing to them, because it can be implemented in less time than the in-house developed software. Also, it will be more cost effective, more efficient, and more reliable. The availability of such software can have favourable impact on the computer utilisation in the developing countries.

A wide variety of application and system software packages are available, but data base management software packages are the most popular ones, these days. In conclusion, the demand for packaged software is going to increase in the near future. In particular, the demand for data base management and communication or networking packages – a software package used to communicate with other systems – will be very high.

4.7 FUTURE OUTLOOK

Advances in software will be slower than those in hardware. As always, software will continue to be a bottleneck in computing. There will be an increase in the use of application packages and the need of outside services to develop them. Programming will in general migrate to a higher and higher level. In other words, more programming will be done in fourth-generation languages. That will result in more end-user programming of all types. The use of application generators by professional programmers will also increase.

5 Historical Development of Programming Languages

Nicholas A. Damachi and Jagtar Chaudhry

5.1 INTRODUCTION

This chapter provides an overview of the historical development of programming languages and explains the various software systems for different applications such as operating systems, word processors, electronic spreadsheets, graphics and computer-aided-design and manufacturing. It explains the use of each kind of application and specifies some guidelines and main considerations in selecting a software system. The overview provided is useful to computer users in developing nations to either develop their own software or select software available off-the-shelf. The term off-the-shelf refers to the software that is produced for mass-marketing and provides some standard functions. Word processors and electronic spreadsheets are some examples of these.

5.2 COMPUTER LANGUAGES

As a result of the proliferation of computer languages, it is useful to provide an evolutionary perspective of these languages in order to foster an understanding of past and present trends in computer language development. This section illustrates major features of some commonly used languages, analyses the advantages and limitations of each and develops some guidelines for the selection of an appropriate language.

Computer languages can be classified in many different categories depending upon their use and structure. Table 5.1 shows some of the classifications.

Table 5.2 shows the historical development of computers. Since the first high-level computer language (FORTRAN) invented by John Backus of IBM in 1956, the number of computer languages has

Table 5.1   Classification of computer languages

High-level/ Low-level	A high-level language is more like a natural language, such as German. It is easier to work with and slower in execution. Low-level language is machine or assembly language, used for system programming.
Procedural/ Problem oriented	A procedural language specifies *how* a task is to be accomplished; problem oriented specifies *what* is to be accomplished.
General/ Special-purpose	General purpose languages are suitable for various applications. Special purpose languages are meant for specific applications, e.g. C, Forth for systems programming, LISP for artificial intelligence. In contrast, Pascal is a general-purpose language.
Structured/ Unstructured	Structured language (Pascal and C) encourages logical, systematic programming, is easy to debug and implement. Unstructured (BASIC and FORTRAN) is the opposite of structured language.
Compiled/ Interpreted	A compiled language program is translated into machine language by the compiler and then executed. An interpreter interprets the program as it reads it line by line and executes it, which makes it comparatively slow.

increased greatly. Today we have around 200 distinct computer languages.

5.3   BASIC

BASIC was designed by Dartmouth professors John G. Kemeny and Thomas Kurtz by incorporating features of FORTRAN and ALGOL to be simple to learn, inexpensive to implement and easy to use. BASIC stands for Beginner's All-purpose Symbolic Instruction Code and well serves its purpose for beginners until programs written in BASIC become too complex and long. It is very easy to learn and easy to dislike.

BASIC is usually provided free, often on a ROM (read only memory) with most of the personal computers. It is available in both

Table 5.2   *Historical development of computer languages*

1980	ADA
	FORTH
	C
	PASCAL
1970	
	APL
	BASIC, PL/1
1960	COBOL, ALOGUL, LISP
	FORTRAN
1950	

interpreted and compiled versions. The interpreted version, though 30 to 50 times slower than a similar compiled program in FORTRAN or Pascal, is quite convenient to write, modify and correct. One can start from writing a simple program in BASIC and extend it by the hit-and-miss approach which is encouraged by BASIC. It makes it so easy to learn BASIC in a haphazard manner that the language has developed a reputation for fostering bad programming habits. The use of the GOTO statement is very common in BASIC which makes it very hard to debug and modify a long and complex program.

BASIC has been around for a number of years and makes available most of its microcomputers powerful string manipulations, single and double precision and other transcendental functions. All kinds of application programs are available in BASIC ranging from business to engineering and scientific application, word-processing to database and file management systems.

5.4   FORTRAN

FORTRAN was developed by John Backus of IBM in 1956. It was the first high-level language. It was developed for solving problems in mathematics, science and engineering, though it has spread in business and education and is widely taught in universities and colleges. FORTRAN is short for FORmula TRANslation. Its statements, syntax and grammar are very similar to mathematical formulas. Arithmetic operations and evaluation of expressions are straightforward. String manipulation is slightly cumbersome. Database management systems, though not very convenient, have been written and are easily available in this language. A huge library of mathematical functions and routines is available to any FORTRAN user. Its modular structure encourages the writing of separate subroutines and functions which can be compiled and tested separately. FORTRAN has a very strong base and has been implemented on almost every mainframe and minicomputer and is gaining ground on microcomputers.

FORTRAN is very prone to typographical errors, which can result in its producing incorrect results in an apparently error-free program. Its column-oriented nature is very irritating. The programs also have a cryptic quality because it allows only six character names for programs, functions and variables.

5.5   PASCAL

Pascal was designed by Nikalus Wirth, a professor in Zurich, Switzerland and named after the French mathematician Blaise Pascal. It is a highly structured computer language that makes large programs easy to design, implement, test, debug and maintain. It is an ideal language for teaching students good programming skills. Pascal programs are made up of smaller programs, each of which itself is a structured program. Pascal variables and subprograms can be named with a high degree of flexibility which makes Pascal programs easy to read. Since all variables and their types must be declared in the beginning, Pascal programs tend to be error-free and easy to modify. Its data types such as records, arrays, pointers and files are very flexible. Pascal has a variety of control structures used to direct a program's order of execution. It has very powerful statements such as Repeat-Until, While-Do and Case. These features permit the user to develop powerful, flexible and structured programs.

The powerful characteristics of Pascal make it relatively unsuitable for small programs. Pascal has limited input/output statements as compared to BASIC. Pascal also needs more computer memory and is more expensive to implement.

5.6   C

C was created in Bell Laboratories originally for in-house systems programming on Bell Lab's Unix operating system in 1972. A language by the name B (after Bell Labs) was developed in-house. B language never came out of Bell Labs. The authors of C, Brian

Kernighan and Dennis Richie named their language C because it followed language B.

C has become very popular for systems programming such as operating systems, compilers, word-processors and other utilities. C makes it very easy to transfer programs between computers with different processors, while still making use of the specific features of particular machines and producing efficient, compact and fast programs. C is both a high-level and low-level language. Like Pascal it is highly structured and has very powerful statements. Like assembly language it is very easy to manipulate bits and bytes in C. It is also called a middle-level language since it falls between assembly language and a high level language.

C is a very compact language with only around 30 reserved keywords. This small core makes C portable and easy to implement. C is made up almost entirely of functions. Each function is stored in standard libraries. Input/Output functions which tend to vary between hardwares are stored in such libraries, thus totally isolating the difference between various versions of C.

C and operating system Unix are closely associated. The Unix operating system is written in C which makes Unix a portable operating system. The combination of C and Unix gives speed, portability and a comfortable working environment.

5.7   OTHER COMPUTER LANGUAGES

Some of the other popular computer languages are Ada, Forth, Lisp, Logo and Modula-2.

Forth is a modern language created by the astronomer Charles Moore in 1975 to control telescopes. It is very compact and fast. Like C it maintains a system library of commands which can be extended depending upon the programming applications.

Ada is a structured language designed and promoted by the United States Department of Defense. It has most of the features of Pascal. Since the Department of Defense is behind Ada, it is likely to become very popular on microcomputers.

5.8   RECOMMENDATIONS

The following criteria are recommended in selecting a computer language for your microcomputer:

Table 5.3   Comparative evaluation of computer languages

BASIC	Easy to learn Slow in running Inexpensive to implement Unstructured and cumbersome for long programs Plenty of software available
FORTRAN	Suitable for engineering and scientific applications Fast execution Plenty of software available Unsuitable for file handling Not very structured
Pascal	Highly structured and powerful Fast execution Excellent data types and file handling Not enough software available Expensive to implement Requires more computer memory
C	Highly structured Very fast in execution Powerful data types Excellent for systems programming Input/Output statements are not very high-level Not enough software available Expensive to implement

1. Assess application. Find out the nature and kind of programming required. This will determine execution time and other computer functions such as output and storage.

2. From Table 5.3, select the language with the most features for your requirements.

5.9   DECIDING THE RIGHT OPERATING SYSTEM

Operating systems act as liaisons between the computer's central processing unit and its own little world – peripheral devices, applications software, user commands, and so on. Since their exact nature and functions are difficult to understand, the average end-user would rather forget about operating systems altogether. But the quality and structure of an operating system has a lot to do with computer capabilities.

The leading multiuser operating systems on the market at the present time are Unix and Unix-derivatives like XENIX, developed by Microsoft Corp.; OASIS by Phase 1 Systems; and MP/M, the multiuser version of CP/M, both by Digital Research Inc. Several multiuser vendors offer more than one operating system for their computers. For example, Altos Computer Systems offers Unix, OASIS, MP/M and Xenix.

Phase 1 is extremely aggressive about finding new computers to run OASIS. Computers by North Star, Altos, Cromemco, Dynabyte, the IBM PC, and several other products run OASIS. A word of caution to be considered is that an operating system that runs on a particular microcomputer will not always run that microcomputer's applications software. For example, even though OASIS runs on Tandy Corporation's TRS Model 16, programs written using OASIS on another microcomputer would not necessarily run on it.

Unix was developed about 10 years ago for minicomputers by Bell Laboratories. During the past few years, it became microcomputer compatible. Some computer experts see it becoming the *de facto* standard for multiuser microcomputers while others are quite critical of it because it has so little application software for education and business. Unix is a fine tool for advanced programmers and researchers. A possible concern is that Unix may be too sophisticated for the average user.

The most commonly cited objections of Unix include the following: It is too sensitive to user mistakes; it doesn't give enough help to inexperienced programmers; and that it lacks file and record locking (When a user is changing data in a file, the locking feature prevents anyone else from trying to change the same data simultaneously).

Enhanced versions of Unix provide interface shells so that, if someone presses the wrong button, the machine will let him/her know what happened, instead of erasing. The Unix-enhancements also add help menus and file locking features.

One of the most controversial features of Unix is its 'hierarchial' file-access method. OASIS and MP/M both use the more conventional alphanumeric scheme where each computer, disk drive, file and subfile has a designation such as 'A-1'. In order to obtain a piece of information using this method, the user would look in the file directory and find, say, that data on account X was in subfiles B-23 through B-45, in file 10B, in disk drive 4, computer 8. Most users have trouble keeping track of all these designations.

A major advantage of the Unix scheme is that the machine, not the user, worries about which disk drive, file, and subfile holds what data (control). The directory lists files under user names and worksta-tions, not alphanumeric designations. To obtain information on account X, the user finds out from the directory that the records are located under Jack Smith, workstation Smith (users and workstations often share the same name). The user keys this into the terminal, and the computer locates all available data on the account.

The first MP/M marketed by Digital Research – MP/M-II – was very inefficient. MP/M-86 is quite powerful. Designed for 8-bit micro-computers, MP/M-II is very slow and imposes a 48K limitation on user applications. MP/M-86, developed for 16-bit computers, fea-tures dynamically allocated RAM, password protection, and time-stamps files so the user knows when a file is created, when it was last backed-up or changed, and so on.

5.10   GRAPHICS

Computer graphics can be used in a large number of ways ranging from artistic design to computer-aided design and manufacturing (CAD/CAM). The primary use of computer graphics is to represent data in a visual format that is easily understandable. Data representa-tion can be used for various applications. A company can use it to present sales and advertising plans. Another company may like to view stock prices and volume charts on a real-time basis from a central data base. Computers may be very useful in drawing pie-charts and line-charts. These charts can be linked to a data base management system or an electronic spreadsheet.

In developing countries, the majority of the data is represented either in numerical or in textual form, which is very time-consuming. Additionally, it does not provide the clarity and understandability that a visual image does. As computers are becoming easily available, some of the standard graphics packages could be used for various graphical applications.

Selecting a graphics package

In selecting a graphics package, the computer output options must be evaluated. Output options include slides, transparencies, hard copy, horizontal and vertical plots, multiple charts per page, integrated text and graphics, and colour. The program should have a menu-driven approach and on-screen help should be available. The term menu-driven refers to a feature provided by the software where the functions available are displayed on the screen and the user selects the desired function. In on-screen help, the user can press a certain key on the keyboard and the software provides a displayed explanation of the functions to be performed. This makes it very easy to learn how to use the software. Editing, sorting and retrieving charts should be simple and flexible. While refining or updating a graph, the software should provide the ability to make changes in size, colour and location of the text. Sophisticated systems can adjust the layout of the text and graph areas automatically. The option of displaying a graph on the screen or producing a hard copy is useful. Good documentation for a graphics package is essential. It should include a catalogue of charts that this software can produce.

5.11   SPREADSHEETS

An electronic spreadsheet is a computerised equivalent of an accountant's worksheet. It is a grid of rows and columns that enables one to organise information in a standardised and easily understandable format. A spreadsheet replaces the tedious work of a pencil and calculator. It is used in preparing budgets, evaluating proposals, comparing alternatives and measuring results. As compared to a manual worksheet, an electronic spreadsheet is very flexible, less error prone and much faster. It can increase productivity and efficiency substantially. In developing countries, an electronic spreadsheet may be used as a handy tool in various areas such as preparing budgets and projections and selecting alternatives.

An electronic spreadsheet works with data in a tabular format which is very convenient in day-to-day operations. Its ability to analyse 'what if' situations, and project and evaluate alternatives makes it a very powerful tool. By changing the input parameters, the changes ripple through the table and recalculated values of variables are displayed. Lotus 1-2-3, VisiCalc and SuperCalc are some of the popular spreadsheets on microcomputers.

The following are the primary considerations in selecting a spreadsheet package:

It should have powerful commands so that it may provide flexibility and versatility.

It should be menu-driven.
On-screen help should be available.
Larger data capacity per cell.
Larger spreadsheet size (number of rows and columns).
Faster speed of calculation.
Automatic and manual calculation.
Flexible cursor control for data entry.

5.12 WORD PROCESSING

As computers are becoming more and more easily available, the time-consuming and tedious task of typewriting is being replaced by word processors. Very powerful and versatile word processor packages are available on a complete range of computers, ranging from home-computers to mainframes. Various features offered by the word processors have made them extremely popular.

The following are some of the features of a good word processing program:

Word Wrap   This means that while typing, when the end of a line is reached, the next word automatically begins at the start of the next line and one does not have to hit a carriage return. The program automatically pulls the rest of the letters from the last word to the next line so that the word is not broken.

Search   By giving a command from the keyboard, the user can search for a particular word or a sentence that occurs in the text.

Search and Replace   Here, a user can search for a word or other character string for any number of occurrences and replace it by another word or character string. This is extremely helpful in correcting spelling errors.

Block operation   This allows a user to mark or identify certain blocks or segments of the text and perform different operations on them. It can allow one to copy a block from one part of the text to another part, or move a block, or delete a block of text.

Insert and Delete   Any word processing program will let one insert or delete characters and/or lines anywhere in the text. This also requires that the word processor have a free moving cursor, which means that one should be able to move the cursor to the left, right, up or down.

Forward and backward scanning   A good word processor lets you scan the text on the screen, and brings forward the previous or following page at the touch of a function key or cursor key.

Formatting Capabilities   Flexible formatting capabilities are extremely crucial. They should let the user select the page length, right and left margins, tabs and decimal tabs and right margin justification. Automatic page numbering and centring are also highly desirable.

An increasing number of word processors are offering spelling checking capabilities. These software dictionaries are extremely useful for proofreading. Another powerful program that makes word processing very easy is a thesaurus program. At the touch of a key, it can flash on the screen as many as ten synonyms for thousands of common English words. Some of the popular word processors on microcomputers are WordStar, Volkswriter and Microsoft Word.

5.13   COMPUTER-AIDED-DESIGN AND MANUFACTURING (CAD/CAM)

Computer-aided-design (CAD)

Computer-aided-design (CAD) concerns the utilisation of computer systems for the purpose of design and communication of design information. The techniques used are not necessarily unique to CAD, but the combination of computer system characteristics necessary for full realisation of CAD make CAD a special field of computer applications. The CAD application may be divided into two categories:

1. A process of manipulating and analysing information in order to choose options and optimise performance characteristics against a given specification.
2. A process of planning and information exchange, inter-organisation or intra-organisation, to assemble and design necessary manufacturing and design information in an optimum fashion.

Computer-aided-manufacturing (CAM)

CAM is a means through which a computer directs the machining of parts. The design profile or tool path of the part to be made is stored in the computer in the form of a program. This program, rather than the operator directs the machine tool to manufacture the part.

Computer-aided-manufacturing (CAM) has a tremendous impact on production, manufacturing, engineering functions and total manufacturing operations. It reduces the throughput time for the manufacturing function, increases use of standard tools and reduces processing errors and changes. It improves overall manufacturing productivity. It also provides improved management control and an understanding of manufacturing.

The market for CAM has been increasing at around 10 per cent annually. Typical problems associated with CAM are high capital investment and lack of standard software.

Computer-aided-integration (CAI)

Once the stage has been set for CAD and CAM, the next highly desirable step is to integrate the two functions. This would eliminate duplicate technical activities and further reduce the total throughput time. Much of what is being developed today is being done with independent stand-alone systems. One system is used for part design, another for design analysis, another for machine tool controls and still another for materials management. The key to integration is to have a common database underlying both CAD and CAM; make it universally acceptable and retain the value of that data once it is put into digital form. Hence a common database, containing all the data that design, analysis, drafting and manufacturing operations generate and utilise, is highly desirable. The CAD/CAM must also be an integral part of the Management Information System (MIS) of the firm.

Historical developments

Computers have been used for design since the 1950s. Special purpose analogue computers were used as models of systems, which could then be refined for experimentation. In the late 1950s, the term computer-aided-design became recognised due to some work on the SAGE system at the Massachusetts Institute of Technology (USA). The SAGE system produced a display on cathode ray tubes.

Time-sharing and multi-terminal computers make on-line working and interactive computing very economical. From the CAD point of view, it is the multi-access nature of the operating system and not the time-sharing characteristic that is important. Multi-access allows multiple access to files of information and provides the essential basis for integrated information systems.

Interactive terminals permit various design options to be explored and high-speed interactive graphics make it extremely convenient to analyse the output.

Hardware aspects

Most of the early CAD/CAM work was done on dedicated computers. Major problems in picture manipulation have been windowing and rotation of three-dimensional diagrams. Windowing is the ability to divide the terminal screen in two or more sections and run different programs in each section simultaneously. Some of these features have been implemented as hardware options on display units. The dedicated systems provided a display screen as an output device. Various input devices such as light-pens, tracker balls, graphical tablets, etc. have been in use for a long time. Graphics terminals have become very popular in the last few years. Various plotter systems compensate for the deficiencies of the terminals, producing accurate final drawings.

The main disadvantage of stand-alone CAD systems has been the expense. Only large companies or universities could afford them and they have done much of the pioneer work in CAD.

Software aspects

One of the most important criteria in the design of CAD software is portability. The cost of developing software tools and application programs is very high and does not offer much economic benefit. The main advantage of the CAD approach has been the lead time to the finished product, rather than direct reduction in cost. The software systems developed should be able to run on various types of hardware. The most common approach has been the use of FORTRAN as the main language.

CAD on microcomputers

The current generation of CAD systems uses mainframes and mini-computers almost universally. The high cost of hardware has limited the acceptance of CAD/CAM systems and kept the software cost high. Today, CAD systems are being implemented on microcomputers and IBM PC is setting the new design standards. Some of the basic CAD systems are available at an unbelievably low price, as low as $US 1000. The peripherals required to produce graphical images are a little expensive but well within the reach of small companies.

Brief review of CAD software for microcomputers

AutoCAD, the Drawing Processor, and MicroCAD are among the first design and drafting software to be available on 16-bit computers. With these tools, the creation and editing of drawings that took two weeks to finish manually with dedicated equipment costing as much as $US 300 000, can now be done much faster on workstations costing from under $10 000 to $US 40 000. These systems run on IBM PC and compatible machines. The Drawing Processor and AutoCAD are two-dimensional line drawings and drafting packages while MicroCAD is a three-dimensional drawing tool that is more useful for modelling and designing than drafting.

Architects may prefer MicroCAD to the other two programs specifically for creating and representing their ideas to clients. An interior designer may use MicroCAD to present more realistic, three-dimensional models to clients. These programs have limited capabilities as compared to minicomputer CAD systems, but they are affordable for an average user.

5.14   SOFTWARE CHECKLIST

The following are points to consider in purchasing systems and application software, and are of varying importance depending upon whether you intend to write your own programs, or only use standard bought in software packages:

1. What high-level languages such as FORTRAN, COBOL, Pascal, and BASIC are available and are they industry standard, such as FORTRAN-77, or a special version?
2. Is assembly language and debugging software available for programming in machine code?
3. Is a disassembler available to convert machine code back to source language?

4. Are cross-assemblers available so you can write machine code for other brands of CPUs?
5. Do the high-level languages support assembly-level routines?
6. Are emulators available to allow communications or to run the software of different computers?
7. Are special languages available for:
   a. Word processing/text editing
   b. Data base management
   c. Business applications
   d. Industrial applications
8. Are multiuser versions of high-level languages available so many people can simultaneously use the computer?
9. Are real-time operating systems available so that the execution of programs will correlate with the passage of time?
10. Is a batch operating system available for noninteractive programming applications?
11. Do the high-level languages support virtual memory or mass storage units which can be accessed similarly to main memory?
12. How much of the software was written by the vendor's company?
13. Are application packages of software available, and are they written by the computer vendor or others?
14. How much do updates of operating systems and languages cost?
15. Are programs supplied to aid in the conversion of old software to run under the updated operating system and languages?
16. What type of security is there to prevent unauthorised users from getting access to your programs and data?
17. How long has the present version of the software been released, and when will a new version be available?

5.15 SPECIAL SOFTWARE CONSIDERATIONS IN DEVELOPING COUNTRIES

Besides the general software considerations mentioned above, there are some special considerations for developing countries. The following are the major problems that these countries encounter:

1. There is substantially more computer awareness in western countries than in developing countries. Computer awareness makes people more comfortable about buying computers and working with them. Fear of working on the computer is far more prevalent in developing

countries. People believe that pressing the wrong key may erase files and damage the computer. This makes people more resistant to accepting computer systems.

2. Hands-on software and hardware training is not as easily available in developing countries due to limited access to computer systems. For example, in India, electrical and computer engineering programs are quite strong theoretically, but each student cannot get as much hands-on experience in using the computer as can a student in the United States.

3. Due to economic constraints, developing countries cannot afford to have many training programs and seminars for software applications.

Given below are a number of factors that should be specially considered in acquiring software systems for developing nations:

1. Software must be very well documented. The documentation should be more critically analysed if the software is purchased from a foreign country. This is because telephone support will be very inconvenient and expensive and training programs are not easily available.

2. Software must be properly debugged. Software with flaws is likely to increase computer fear and make computers less acceptable.

3. Software should be menu-driven. As explained earlier, menu-driven software is easy to operate and requires less training, and is highly desirable in developing countries.

4. Software must have proper built-in checks for data entry and should accept only valid responses. This feature makes inexperienced users more comfortable in working with the computer.

5. Software should be time-proven. New software may have some bugs which are removed as the software is used. Developing countries are definitely not a good test market for the new software.

References

BEEBY, W., 'The Future of Integrated CAD/CAM Systems: The Boeing Perspective', *IEEE*, Jan 1982.

BREDIN, H., 'Unmanned Manufacturing', *Mechanical Engineering* Feb 1982.

COLE, BERNARD, 'A Family Tree of Computer Languages', *Popular Computing* Sep 1983.

DAMACHI, N. A. and CHAUDHRY, J. 1985 'Future Computer Languages', *Proceedings*, *ISECON* (Dallas, USA).

FOX, DAVID and WAITS, MITCHELL, 'Pascal Primer', (Howard W. Sams Co., 1982).

GATES, WILLIAM, 'Languages Essay', *PC World* Special Edition, 1983/84.

GRAY, STEPHEN, 'Stepping up to Draft-Aide', *PC Magazine* Jan 1984.

MACHRONE, BILL, 'Micro Linguistics: Languages for the PC', *PC Magazine*, Sep 1983.

MILLER, HARRY, 'Introduction to Spreadsheets', *PC World* Aug 1984.

MYERS, W., 'CAD/CAM: The Need for a Broader Focus', *IEEE*, Jan 1982.

RITCHIE, DAVID, 'A CAD System for the People', *PC Magazine* Oct 1984.

SMITH, DAVID, 'Computer-Aided-Design', *PC World* Oct 1983.

WILCOX, DAVID, 'The Boom in Business Graphics', *PC World* Aug 1984.

6 Strategic Management and the Computer

William Holloway and William Lindsay

6.1 INTRODUCTION

It is well known that the environment of the manager in today's world is turbulent, change-oriented, sometimes chaotic, and in need of more systematic ways to deal with significant events. This is particularly true for developing countries given the increased interaction with not only their close neighbouring countries but the developed nations as well. Many managers have developed a sense of frustration about the process required to just adequately deal with the daily demands made on them. A systematic concern for the future and its implications often takes a lower priority because of the press of the moment when in fact a systematic analysis is desperately needed.

The existence of long-range planning models and documents has a rich tradition in business management. This planning process is a result of the need for stability and predictability in the use of resources as a remedy for dealing with a turbulent environment.

Large and complex organisations have long recognised the importance and, in fact, the survival need for long-range planning. There is more involved here than just long-range planning however. Some important questions intrude. For example, what major new products or services will my competitors offer to our mutual potential customers next year? Have I taken into account government regulatory changes which will affect my company? What technological changes in my industry offer opportunities that I could take advantage of? and on it goes. All such questions lie outside the boundaries of operational long-range planning. In the unsystematic approach often taken, or forced upon some managers, such questions cause frustration. Often the frustration is compounded by the knowledge that these questions exist while little, seemingly, can be done to deal with them.

Strategic management accomplishes several things which tend to lower the frustration level.

1. A systematic approach is taken to examining the company.
2. Priorities can be established for the long run use of resources.
3. Specific environmental threats and opportunities can be identified.
4. Specific strengths and weaknesses of the company are isolated.
5. Significant events, which could have a positive or negative impact on the performance of the firm, can be more readily identified and weighed.
6. Confidence in the manager's decisions may be significantly enhanced.

The computer can be of significant help in processing the data needed to obtain these advantages. The next section will outline a method for developing a strategic management system and will show how the computer can be used to integrate seemingly unrelated data to provide vital information needed for this process.

Managers in developing countries will find that utilisation of the computer provides a number of benefits. Included among these are:

(a)   Better utilisation of time because of more rapid access to data
(b)   Greater confidence in the decisions made from information developed
(c)   Reduced space requirements for filing, notes, etc.

These factors and many more will become apparent as the computer capability of the manager increases.

6.2   STRATEGIC MANAGEMENT

Adoption of a strategic management approach requires use of the following three elements:

First, an organisation must determine its basic purpose and state that purpose in operational terms. This implies that there must be sufficient reason to allocate valuable resources, both human and material, to the job of producing goods or services of this firm.

Second, there must be some appropriate structure of relationships between people and the offices they hold so that the work can be accomplished.

Third, basic sub-systems which drive the survival, stability and growth of the company in terms of its people must be in place and working effectively. These sub-systems include communication, rewards and punishment, decision networks, and various levels of goals and objectives. Because of the broad nature of these elements, top, middle and first-line managers are compelled to think in strategic as well as operational long range terms about the organisation if recognition is to be given to these subsystems.

For example, if the textile industry finds that changing technology is providing new fibres at much lower cost and much higher quality, the impact of this change must be assessed. If a textile manufacturer in a developing country has a basic purpose of supplying inexpensive clothing to a wide market and a limited price customer group, it is important to determine just how this new technology will impact on the firm. The immediate opportunity might suggest a broadening of the customer base to include higher priced clothing. This should be done on the basis of the availability of the technology only if such a stratagem is compatible with the purpose of the firm as expressed in its mission statement.

If this opportunity is not compatible with the organisational mission, it is quite likely that the firm will have difficulty integrating the new approach into the existing organisational framework. This is often seen in the approach of the marketing segment of the firm to new types of customers.

Many times the distribution channels for lower priced products are uniquely suited to the sale of such products all through the distribution network. When a new type of product is introduced that is to be purchased by a different segment of the market, a different distribution process is involved. It is possible that the sales people do not understand the needs of the new type of customer and are unable to be effective in making the marketing delivery system function in the optimum way.

In this context the people and the offices they hold in the company may be critical. A sales manager unable to understand a new type of customer will not be effective in leading the sales force to obtain the necessary business, promotional arrangements, and personal relationships so essential to the bargaining process.

This in turn can influence the internal subsystems in many ways. For example, the establishment of sales incentives may be based on unrealistic goals because management is unfamiliar with this new area of customer, distribution network and promotional arrangements.

The problem that most managers encounter is the very practical one of converting abstract, long-range mission statements and goals into specific steps which will be taken in the short run, i.e., tomorrow when the work day begins. In the next section, a method is presented for solving this daunting but surmountable problem.

6.3   DAY-TO-DAY MANAGEMENT VERSUS STRATEGIC MANAGEMENT

To establish a link between the abstract premises of long range strategy and the action steps of today's work, we must clarify the difference between strategic activities and ordinary, routine operational management activities. If the manager can say 'I am confident that the things I am doing in the daily running of my business generally reflects the accomplishment of my basic objectives as outlined in the overall long range goals for this organisation', that manager is running the business in a way which will successfully blend the short-term and long-term interests of the firm. In other words, the manager is at least attempting to operate his part of the organisation strategically.

Through the use of the computer, today's manager finds it possible to obtain much higher levels of analysis for strategic implementation than in the past. This will be discussed in more detail below under the sections on MIS (Management Information Systems) and DSS (Decision Support Systems).

6.4   THE PROCESS OF STRATEGIC MANAGEMENT

There are several basic steps involved in the development of a strategic management process. A number of authors have outlined the steps in this process and all seem to follow a similar pattern. The following steps will reflect the work of Glueck[1] and the authors of this material as well as others who have contributed to the development of strategic management theory.

The first step is to determine the kind of business the organisation is or wants to be, along with the development of a mission statement and a relatively detailed account of 'who we are' and 'what market we wish to serve'. Also, the values of the top management must be made clear, since, even if they remain unstated, they will play a significant part in the development of the strategy. Porter[2] summarised this strategy formulation phase of the strategic management process using these three basic questions:

1. What is the business doing now?
2. What is happening in the environment?
3. What should the business be doing?

An example of an effective, operational mission statement might be the following:

> We are manufacturers of low priced clothing. We provide our customer a limited line of products of outer wear in a temperate climate for practical work use. Our designs are conservative and utilitarian to appeal to a broad range of users within a relatively narrow income range. It is our purpose to maintain a low price so that our consumer will always be able to obtain the selection desired without being burdened by high cost. We intend to provide no 'frills' but long life and good quality must be a standard on which our customer can depend.

This relatively simple statement delimits the area to be served and sets boundaries for decision-making. This company would not spend research and development resources on high priced clothing products for a luxury market. It would not, for example, test market high fashion designer blue jeans because the market and profit potential seemed attractive.

The idea here is that the mission statements and purposes of the organisation serve to aid the decision-making process when other opportunities or threats appear which could influence strategic thinking. This is not to say that a mission statement is stagnant or unchangeable. But it must be recognised that there are consequences for changing it.

The second major step in the strategic management process is to make an evaluation of the total environment in which the organisation exists. This analysis and evaluation consists of two parts. First, the major components and issues which make up the environment must be clarified and an assessment of the external threats and opportunities must be made. Second, the internal strengths and weaknesses of the company must be analysed and evaluated. As we will see below, this systematic evaluation and analysis can benefit dramatically from the use of the speed and power of the computer.

The analysis consists of breaking down the organisation's environment into external and internal environmental components. Each component must be ranked in terms of its importance in relation to the other components and also in terms of its potential influence on the future of the organisation. A specific example will be developed in a later section. Now, we will consider the factors to be assessed in the external environment of organisations.

6.5 THE EXTERNAL ENVIRONMENT

Glueck[3] has listed six elements or factors which must be analysed in the external environment: economic, government/legal, market competitive, supplier/technological, geographic, and social/other.

Economic

In this category, all aspects of economic life for the business should be considered. If the economy is in an expansion period there may be new opportunities. For example, if interest rates are high, planning for costs of business investment may need to be realigned. What about tax rates? If our company operates in several countries, what effect will exchange rate fluctuations have on our prices? All of these factors and questions must be considered strategically, that is, as long range and external factors affecting the company.

Government/legal

Government plays several roles which influence the company. Government also operates at several levels and thus must be analysed at each level to understand the different ways it can influence the business.

A major role of government is that of lawmaker. Managers must be continually aware of the various legislative acts which influence the business.

Another role is that of purchaser. Government may buy many goods and services and in that sense be a customer providing economic opportunity. As government policies change, the outcome may require new threats or opportunities to be assessed.

Market/competitive

The external environment in this category exerts several pressures on the organisation. Of primary concern, particularly for consumer goods companies, are the demographic characteristics of age, income and population. Obviously, if the number of people change, their age distribution becomes older (or younger), and their incomes tend to vary; it is critical to the success of any organisation to be able to assess these changes.

If the number of competitors increases, or a new product is introduced by a competitor, the organisation must be prepared to analyse such new data in light of its own plans and forecasts.

Supplier/technological

To develop a sound strategy, the availability of raw materials, technology, and services which must be purchased from outside the firm have to be assessed. In the case of suppliers, it is necessary to determine the number of suppliers available to determine one's basic leverage position. If there are few suppliers, it is possible that larger inventories and longer lead times will be required. In addition, depending on the bargaining position of the company, it may need to allocate larger amounts of available cash to anticipate price fluctuations.

Technologically, the industry may be more (or less) complex. In either case, analysis of the importance of this aspect of the external environment is needed. In high technology industries, market fluctuations may be great unless a few proprietary processes or ideas are 'owned' by a few companies which are able to maintain stability due to their dominant position in a narrow market segment.

Geographic

Opportunities must be analysed in view of their geographic location to insure that productivity and/or sales goals can be effectively met. Establishing sales territories, location of production plants, service centres and sources of supply can play a vital role in the strategy of a company.

Social

In any society there are basic values held by the people of that society which directly influence a business. As societies evolve, they frequently modify their values. Businesses must be prepared to recognise these changes if they are to be successful. For example, the supply of workers with the appropriate skills available may be influenced by their particular values regarding overnight travel or leaving home or city. If family considerations are valued more strongly than job considerations and career opportunities located elsewhere, a company may not be able to acquire the kinds of talent needed to run the business in outlying areas. However, if the economy takes a downturn and job availability is critical people may be willing to alter their values if a job, career or subsistence is at stake. Thus, it can be seen that a business must be keenly aware of the importance of social values to its productivity and long term strategic objectives.

6.6 EXTERNAL ENVIRONMENT DATA ANALYSIS

After the major environmental factors have been analysed, they must be categorised and prioritised in some way. This is where the judgement of the strategist is useful. Only the person responsible for the long range strategy of the organisation is in a position to make this kind of assessment.

Weighting

Once the major factors in the environment which can influence the development of strategy have been established, a diagnosis of the factors in terms of their importance can occur. Weighting is a useful way to establish relative priorities for each of the environmental factors in relation to each other as they now appear to influence the strategy of the company.

To apply the weighting scheme, arbitrary values for each factor must be set. Almost any set of values may be used to provide a standardised calibration over some relevant range. For example, values of plus 5 through 0 to minus 5 might be chosen.

Using these numbers, an environmental factor which was most important in moving the organisation in a positive way would be valued as a +5. Conversely, a factor which clearly would have negative influence on the company's strategy in some significant way could have a −5 rating. For example, a company which makes products dependent on the availability of disposable income of its population of customers might foresee a downturn in the economy which would create significant unemployment. This, in turn, would possibly result in decreased investment opportunities with concurrent higher costs for companies making these products. The importance of such economic downturns on this firm would require a heavy negative weighting, such as −5 for this factor.

If a factor does not seem to influence the environment relative to the other factors being considered it might receive a 0 weighting. This does not mean the factor is unimportant, but that relative to the other factors being considered its weighting is neutral at this time in considering any important change in resource use.

An example of a positive weighting situation might be a marketing-oriented consumer goods company with a new proprietary product in a growing market. This new product might be one which lends itself well to the distribution network and is known, based on extensive test market research, to be highly acceptable to a large consumer population. Marketing/competitive factors could conceivably have a +5 weighting in relation to the other factors being considered because of the potentially strong position of the new product in the marketplace.

The distinction between weightings can be developed into a more complex scale. For example, at the discretion of the strategist, decimal points may be added to increase the level of discrimination. Subsets might be added to further clarify the factor with weight and impact factors assigned. In addition, more than one factor may be given the same rating. The main point to remember is that this procedure provides value oriented data to decision-makers so that the resources of the company may be better utilised.

Impact

Impact is defined as the influence and importance of a given factor in the future, but within the time frame of the strategic plan. This might be from three to five years.

Again a numbering scheme is used to assess relative value. Glueck[4] has used +50 through 00 to −50. Whatever scheme is used the breadth of the calibration is an arbitrary one.

Using the examples developed in the section on weighting, each factor can now be analysed for impact.

Table 6.1

Factor	Weighting	Impact
Economic	4	35
Government/Legal	4	30
Marketing/Competitive	2	40
Supplier/Technological	3	20
Geographic	0	00
Social	−1	−25

6.7 ENVIRONMENTAL IMPACT AND WEIGHTING: AN EXAMPLE

Table 6.1 shows a numeric example of the environmental profile of a typical company with weighting and impact rankings.

In our example the strategist apparently has determined that the economic environment of the company presents some positive opportunities. This could be represented by a favourable climate of low taxation, low interest rates for investment and plenty of labour available for employment. This is also reflected in the positive 35 impact. Our strategist, when looking at all other factors concluded that the future for the company is enhanced by this projected economic climate in such a way as to offer possible growth opportunities.

In each case we can see not only the relative position of each factor, but also a cross comparison of the present (weighting) and the future (impact).

There is apparently a warning signal in the negative weighting and impact of the social factor. This may reflect an adverse reaction from some constituency in society to the products of the company. For example, if our company were an ethical pharmaceutical manufacturer, ethical drugs produced for and dispensed by the medical professional which had harmful side effects might present a threat to a group organised to protect society's interests regarding drugs. While this may be an event that is not new and recurs infrequently it still must be given due consideration because of the real or potential use of resources to appropriately deal with the problem. There may be immediate ongoing effects (weighting) and also future threats (impact) to available resources because of law suits, public relations campaigns, etc. The weighting of −1 would indicate only a moderate effect of this factor on the overall strategy of the firm, while the −25 impact weighting indicates an appreciable severity level, should this environmental contingency actually occur.

In examining both the internal and external environment, the computer can be very useful for analysis. The development of strategy is a complex and challenging requirement of business life today. The computer affords the manager a tool which allows for a more definitive array and analysis of relevant data.

The preparation of spreadsheets as discussed elsewhere in this chapter can increase the detail of the analysis. For example if under the economic factor, sub-sets of weighting and impact for labour market, gross national product, interest rates, etc. would enhance the analysis, the computer allows for this complexity while still retaining effectiveness and efficiency. Once the categories have been developed the data can be upgraded periodically, stored for historical record and treated for statistical significance.

6.8 INTERNAL ENVIRONMENT DATA ANALYSIS

As there are specific factors to analyse in the external environment, there are also internal factors which must be considered. This is the second part of the analysis process. Five factors comprise the internal analysis. Glueck[5] lists the five as: financial/accounting, marketing/distribution, production/operations, personnel/labour relations, and corporate resources. Each of these factors is considered in the same analytical way as was discussed in the section on the external environment. Both weighting and impact values are assigned and the resulting comparisons and contrasts made. All except possibly corporate resources have straightforward definitions. In this category some explanation may be appropriate. Glueck suggests that the image and prestige of the company, size in relation to the industry, research and development capacity, effectiveness of management information and computer systems are some of the elements to be considered in this category.

In summary then, considering all of the internal factors the central question is: What are the ways that the company can capitalize on its strengths and minimize the influence of its weaknesses to improve the effectiveness of its strategy?

Information systems in strategy formulation

Strategy formulation is an information-driven process. This is probably due to the great amount of uncertainty which is common to the process. Galbraith[6] stated it in this fashion:

> The basic proposition is that the greater the uncertainty of the task, the greater the amount of information that has to be processed in the execution of the task. If the task is well understood prior to performing it, much of the activity can be pre-planned. If it is not understood, then during the actual task execution, more knowledge is learned, which leads to changes in resource allocations, schedules and priorities. All these changes require information processing during task performance. Therefore, the greater the task uncertainty, the greater the amount of information that must be processed in order to insure effective performance.

A brief history of corporate planning models will show how computer-aided approaches to strategic planning have changed over the past 25 years.[7]

Some of the problems experienced in the development of corporate planning models in the US and other countries may provide some information on pitfalls which can be avoided by developing countries. A few of these problems were encountered because of the newness of computers and the corporate planning techniques which were being developed to use their capabilities. Others were due to the inability of those developing the models to anticipate the true effects of use of the models prior to their installation. Because of the current stage of development, managers in developing countries may be able to take advantage of lessons learned in developing prior systems, thus avoiding many of the previous problems. Simple, but powerful computer programs which could be used in developing countries to model corporate planning approaches are now becoming available for use on micro-computers, as well as larger computing machines.

Before 1963, corporate planning models were being developed using a 'bottom-up' approach. This simply meant that the company would develop data about costs, sales, product introductions and other variables, construct a computer model that would show trends in the variables and attempt to analyse their impact on the firm. They were generally written in assembler or FORTRAN programming languages. The former language was very basic, but not very powerful.

It took many instructions to develop a workable planning model, but was more efficient to run on the computer. FORTRAN was a powerful, scientific computer language which was easier to use but was less efficient to run on the computer.

Although these early models were designed to represent the entire organisation, with what was called a 'total systems' approach, they were generally rigid and inflexible, lacking any method for changing basic assumptions.

From 1963 to 1973, modelling approaches changed significantly. A top-down approach, starting with strategic targets, such as return on investment and market share goals, was used. Forecasting became popular. Simulation language development permitted testing of decision assumptions with 'what-if' questions. These languages were written especially for the purpose of developing models of the firm and segments of its operations. Once the models were developed, assumptions, such as an increase or decrease in sales or costs could be entered into the program, and decision-makers could observe the effects on the model in terms of changes in capacity, overall costs or profits. In this way, a manager could ask, for example, 'What if I increased sales by 5 per cent and decreased cost by 10 per cent over the next 3 years?'

From 1974 to 1980, more changes in modelling were made. The use of forecasts as a starting point for the model was questioned, resulting in attempts to more carefully integrate into the models financial and non-financial assumptions. Models were redesigned to be more user-oriented, take advantage of development of more powerful simulation languages and provide for the opportunity to analyse a 'portfolio' of Strategic Business Units (SBU's) to determine overall decision impacts on the firm.

The early 1980s have extended the search for more precise methods for optimising SBU portfolio decisions and for using microcomputers to improve intermediate-term decisions of top and middle managers as they attempt to implement their long-term strategy.

Porter's[8] three basic strategy formulation questions, mentioned previously, have made the use of computers more and more important in the development of strategic management systems. With an effective management information system (MIS), many of the problems of assessing what is happening in the internal environment of the firm can be overcome. A different type of system must be developed to gather, process and assess the environmental data which must be turned into strategic information for decision-makers, who must be aware of 'What is happening in the environment?'. Finally, the question of 'What should the business be doing?' requires the ability to access data, develop an appropriate model, and ask 'What if . . . ?' questions to assess the impact of critical variables on the strategy of the company. None of these are easy systems to develop, but they can make the task of strategy development much simpler and more effective. The above discussion becomes very pertinent if one considers what is happening to some companies in developing countries, such as Nigeria, today. They are closing down because of unanticipated foreign exchange problems. Perhaps the most noticeable weakness has been these companies' failure to develop processes that rely on locally available materials, rather than those purchased from foreign sources. These problems might have been foreseen, and perhaps avoided, by the proper use of strategic planning techniques.

The more accurate the information that is available to the manager for determining the answers to these three vital questions, the more likely it is that effective strategic planning and strategic management will be done. Let us examine three sources from which information to answer these questions can be obtained. We will then explain how information systems and technology can make the job of gathering and analysing this critical information easier.

6.9   THE SOURCES OF STRATEGIC INFORMATION

Management information systems

The use of MIS has become a near-necessity in companies of any appreciable size in the US, Europe, Japan and most of the other developed countries. Early uses of computers were to handle financial transactions, track inventory, manage production and analyse sales. Operating managers found computers were a tremendous aid in managing countless details of day-to-day operations, which had previously required many people and much time to generate less than accurate reports.

Today, the frontiers in information systems at the operating level lie in the challenge of integrating the many streams of information which are now available into a single, controllable unit. Such units, on the shop floor of a manufacturing firm would be capable of directing numerous machines and operations from a single 'nerve centre', or control area.

Although much of the information gathered in the course of using the MIS is used for immediate decision-making of an operational nature, a significant portion may also prove to be useful in strategic decision-making, as well. For example, analysis of current financial ratios and performance can provide the basis on which to develop future strategies and to set goals for improvement.

Use of the computer for environmental scanning

A challenging and perplexing problem for managers is to obtain adequate, timely information about the surrounding environment which is becoming more and more complex. The components of the environment such as economic, governmental, market/competitive, etc., have been discussed above. Timely information must be gathered if the type of environmental analysis that has been detailed in this chapter is to be done. The challenge comes in locating the data that is needed and in transforming that data into useful information.

Until recently, managers in the US had to laboriously gather their own data, or attempt to use governmental data, which may not have been suited to their needs. Compatibility between computers and computer formats was often a major problem. Today, there are a number of 'information utilities' which have large statistical data bases. The data bases are continuously updated with information on economic, social, political and technological changes which are taking place in the environment. Managers can 'subscribe' to receive data from these utilities. They can then obtain direct communications access into the data base which is of interest to them. Information can be picked off or 'downloaded' into the firm's computer, where it can be used to guide strategic decision-making.

Although the development and use of information sharing through common data bases has been a phenomenon which is unique to developed countries, the potential for their development and use in third-world countries is indeed great. Several steps will probably be required before such data bases are available for common use. Some standardisation of reporting procedures will have to be agreed on by countries, perhaps on a regional basis. Some agency, public or private, will have to be set up to gather, process and disseminate the data. Finally, and perhaps most important, companies will have to be approached and convinced that it is in their best interest to supply data to the agency over a long period of time. This might be approached by pointing to the many benefits obtained in developed countries which have access to such data. Pearce and Robinson[9] recently presented a comprehensive overview of the environmental forecasting process, approaches and a list of information sources, including a number of the 'information utilities' listed above. The process for environmental forecasting which they suggest includes four steps:

1. Selecting the key variables in the environment critical to the firm.
2. Selecting the major sources of environmental information.
3. Evaluating forecasting approaches or techniques.
4. Integrating the results of forecasts into the strategic management process.

Steps 2 and 3 are directly concerned with information needs and sources.

Selection of information sources is driven by the nature of the business, the sophistication of the forecast requirement and the cost of providing needed information *vs.* its perceived benefits.

The forecasting approaches which were listed are well-known and have been discussed at length in such sources as Chambers, *et al.*[10] Some of the forecasting approaches included quantitative techniques of time-series analysis, linear and multiple regression, and econometric models and qualitative techniques of salesforce estimates, juries of executive opinion, market research, scenarios, Delphi technique and brainstorming.

While these techniques are known to professional forecasters and analysts, their use may be mysterious to general managers who have not been introduced to them. A brief explanation of the conditions under which they can be applied may prove to be informative.

Time-series analysis is of use in short or medium-range planning, where there are regular, predictable variations in sales or production levels as a result of annual occurrences of holidays, seasons or other patterns. Linear and multiple regression and econometric models are developed in a similar fashion to time-series analysis by taking past data, developing mathematical expressions to fit the major part of that data and testing out the mathematical model to see if it can be used to predict the future direction of the business.

The qualitative approaches do not try to forecast future performance of a business by using past data. Instead, they rely on various types of judgement to solve problems, make decisions and prepare plans for the future. Salesforce estimates and juries of executive opinion are most often used to estimate the sales level or future condition of a company. Market research is conducted to determine how a customer will react to a new product or thinks of an existing product. Scenarios are alternative plans for a company's use, depending on which set of environmental conditions is likely to prevail during a specified time. The Delphi Technique is applied by having various experts to assess the likelihood of a specific event taking place, such as discovery of a cure for cancer or high blood pressure, and the impact of that event on a firm, a country or the world. Finally, brainstorming is a technique used to solve unstructured, often future-oriented problems, by having a group of people propose various creative alternatives to be investigated for feasibility.

The techniques discussed above range in cost and complexity from high to low and must be carefully evaluated before being used. Table 6.2 (at the end of the chapter on page 101) summarizes these techniques and factors.

It is particularly interesting to note that there are now companies and consultants specialising in environmental forecasting for countries and regions around the world. Such consultants are especially valuable for companies operating in politically unstable countries or regions, where environmental changes such as government turmoil, nationalisation and unfavourable regulation can have a major impact on business results or plans. Some of the firms and their 'products' include:

1. Haner's Business Environmental Risk Index (monitors 15 economic and political variables in 42 countries).
2. Frost & Sullivan's World Political Risks Forecasts (predicts the likelihood of various catastrophes befalling an individual company).
3. Probe International's custom reports for specific companies (examines broad social trends).

Decision support systems

Perhaps the newest use for computer technology in strategy development is its use as the basis for 'decision support systems' (DSS). Managers at the top and middle management levels have little need for operating level information when they are involved in strategic planning and decision-making activities. What they need is a 'tool' to aid them in assessing the impact of decisions on their firm. For example, 'If I raise prices by 5 per cent, how much additional profit will it generate if certain costs increase 3 per cent and others increase 10 per cent?' This type of 'tool' for asking 'What if?' questions, based on a model of the firm and its environment is becoming more and more accessible to top and middle managers in large, medium and small firms, as we shall see below. King[11] discussed the concept of strategic decision support systems (SDSS). He pointed out that models and approaches such as DSS and Artificial Intelligence and other information systems are 'quantitatively, not qualitatively, different from other more familiar varieties of models'.

Artificial intelligence can be briefly described as an attempt to make computers duplicate decision-making processes which have been previously considered by many people to be capable of being done only by humans. For example, some medical diagnostic procedures have now been programmed to operate on computers so that a patient's symptoms may be entered and a highly accurate suggested diagnosis may be output. This has been made possible in the last several years by faster computer operating speeds and newer and more creative programming techniques.

Basically, SDSS is 'specifically designed to support top management and planners in their strategic management functions'. It typically uses more highly aggregated data than an MIS system, and its output is formatted for the decision-making tasks of long-range planners.

King[12] gave the names of some companies reported to have developed SDSS systems, such as RCA, Citibank, Louisiana National Bank, American Airlines, and First National Bank of Chicago. He also provided some interesting examples of the advantages of using SDSS systems. One firm developed its cost information system to a high degree and then used the resulting information to provide a superior pricing strategy for its products, supported by a promotional and sales incentive system which gave it a significant competitive edge over its rivals. Another firm built a model which allowed it to accurately assess competitors' strategy and to react appropriately to anticipated changes. A third company developed carefully timed product changes based on information about new and changing technology.

In developing countries, where volatile changes in demand for products, such as oil, take place regularly, the use of SDSS could help to reduce uncertainty to more manageable levels. This planning approach would at least permit contingency plans to be made, so that when a major downturn or upturn in demand arrived, the organisation would be prepared to take action and to anticipate the effects which would be likely to follow from such action. Similar contingency plans could be made, and their effects assessed through an SDSS model for the strategic factors of currency fluctuations, raw materials shortages or work stoppages due to strikes or other turmoil.

6.10 INFORMATION SYSTEMS FOR STRATEGIC PLANNING

Hardware and software for strategic management

Hardware has been developed much more rapidly over the past ten years than has the software to take advantage of the increased capability of the new technology. Hardware has included two basic technological components – integrated circuits and communications systems.

Integrated circuits have permitted expanded memory and greater operating speeds to be attained than ever before. This has been done while reducing both the cost and size of the computer and computer peripheral devices.

Communication systems have been developed which take advantage of integrated circuit technology to transmit data over long distances via conventional wires, microwave and space satellite modes. Once again, because of economies of scale, this has resulted in lower and lower costs being incurred per unit of information. It also makes possible the use of common data bases by planners in many parts of the company, who may be separated geographically by hundreds or thousands of miles.

The end result of low cost hardware and readily available communication channels for accessing and transferring data, has been to encourage widespread use of sophisticated planning approaches in most companies. Boulton *et al.*[13] found that 86 per cent of respondents to a long-range planning survey of corporate planning executives in the US and Canada taken in 1979, were using some type of written, formal planning process. At least part of the reason for this upsurge in planning is due to the availability of computers and information needed to plan more effectively. The same survey showed that 61 per cent of the respondents were using computers and/or corporate planning models in their planning process.

Software has not kept pace with hardware in rapidity of development, nor has there been an appreciable decline, if any, in the price of software. Nevertheless, software has been designed which permits easier gathering, analysis and use of computer technology for strategic management. Strides have been made in both general purpose and special purpose software. General purpose software includes 'spreadsheet', database management and graphics presentation programs. Special purpose programs are those which have been designed especially for strategic management applications, or even more narrowly, for a specific industry such as drug manufacturers or hospitals.

Some of the early developers of decision support systems introduced modelling 'languages' such as IFPS (Execucom), Express (Management Decision Systems) and FCS-EPS (EPS, Inc.). According to Horwitz,[14] they envisaged their systems being used by financial and market research analysts, rather than general managers. However, because of the interactive nature of DSS, it became easier for the user to develop 'hands-on' capability, rather than trying to translate his or her needs for information and analysis to an analyst who was not familiar with the user's information needs or mode of operation.

An example of one of the most sophisticated attempts to develop a computer model for integrated long, medium and operational planning is found in the case of Texas Instruments' 'MODPLAN' system described in a case study by Boulton and Kight:

> MODPLAN is a management data base system for collecting, consolidating, and reporting of numerical information. MODPLAN was developed to help TI managers, planners, and analysts do their jobs easier and better. More specifically, it provides a tool which allows computer power to be applied to the tasks of collection, manipulation, analysis and reporting of any numerical data which can be arranged by time periods, such as is commonly done in forecasting, planning, budgeting, reporting and controlling activities.[15]

Although not described in detail, the descriptions of the applications of MODPLAN by managers at Texas Instruments leads one to believe that MODPLAN is a highly sophisticated 'spreadsheet' or database management system, but not a true SDSS, as King defined it. Two of MODPLAN's apparent limitations are its capability to store data (only 175 lines can be stored out of the 512 total lines available in MODPLAN.) and the fact that product changes and updates are not easily made due to the nature of the system.

Despite these limitations, MODPLAN is undoubtedly one of today's most comprehensive, sophisticated and widely used corporate planning and control systems in use. Statistics for 1978–79 indicated that the system had about $1.8 million in annual operating costs, was staffed by only 9 people, served 1620 terminals, worldwide, and was accessed annually by users over 4 million times.

Implications for management in third world countries

The planning methods and computer technology currently available in the United States is becoming available internationally. While the limitations of these methods and technologies must be faced, they can address the unique challenges afforded management in third world nations.

First, the philosophy of planning, presented above, can certainly be adapted to good use in third world firms. Even without the availability of sophisticated computer hardware and software, systematic strategic planning and management can pay excellent dividends for sustained users. The process of strategic planning should be established and maintained from the beginning of a firm's life to its finish.

Second, effort should be directed toward identifying information sources which will provide the quantity and quality of information needed for effective strategic decision-making. This means that attention must be focused on developing complete internal information through the MIS system, as well as finding external sources from which to obtain data and/or information about economic, social, political and cultural changes in the organisation's surrounding business environment.

Third, after a viable, systematic approach to planning and information gathering has been established, then attention should be given to hardware and software requirements for processing and analysing needed data. Too often, companies buy hardware and software for data gathering and analysis without thoroughly probing their planning and information needs. They then find themselves underutilising their computer and information resources, failing to integrate their planning process with operations, or simply 'going through the motions' of strategic planning without using the designed plan for decision making.

References

1. William F. Glueck *Business Policy and Strategic Management* (New York: McGraw-Hill Book Company, 1980) pp. 201–2.
2. Michael Porter *Competitive Strategy* (New York: MacMillan-Free Press, 1980).
3. William F. Glueck *Business Policy*, pp. 93–102.
4. *Ibid.*, pp. 117.
5. *Ibid.*, pp. 152–62.
6. Jay Galbraith 'Organization Design: An Information Processing View', in *Organization Planning: Cases and Concepts* Jay W. Lorsch and Paul R. Lawrence. (eds) (Homewood, IL.: R. D. Irwin, Inc., 1972).
7. Richard A. Pappas and Donald S. Remer, *Managerial Planning*, (March/April, 1984): pp. 4–16.
8. Michael Porter *Competitive Strategy*.
9. John A. Pearce and Richard B. Robinson, Jr. 'Environmental Forecasting: Key to Strategic Management,' *Business* (July–September, 1983): pp. 3–12.
10. J. C. Chambers, T. K. Mullick, and D. D. Smith 'How to Choose the Right Forecasting Technique', *Harvard Business Review*, (July–August, 1978).
11. William R. King 'Achieving the Potential of Decision Support Systems', *The Journal of Business Strategy*, (Winter, 1983) pp. 84–91.
12. *Ibid.* p. 87.
13. William R. Boulton, Stephen G. Franklin, William M. Lindsay and Leslie W. Rue 'How Are Companies Planning Now – A Survey' *Long Range Planning*, (February, 1982) pp. 82–6.
14. Elisabeth Horwitz 'DSS: Effective Relief for Frustrated Management', *Business Computer Systems*, (July, 1984) pp. 48–58.
15. William R. Boulton and Charles W. Kight 'Texas Instruments MOD-PLAN (A)', in William R. Boulton, *Business Policy*, (New York: Macmillan and Co., 1984) pp. 567–600.

Table 6.2   Popular Approaches to forecasting

Techniques	Short description	Cost	Popularity	Complexity
Quantitative				
Causal				
Economic models	Simultaneous systems of multiple regression equation	High	High	High
Single and multiple	Variations in dependent variables are explained by variations in the independent one(s)	High	High	Medium
Time series				
Trend extrapolation	Linear exponential S-curve or other types of projections	Medium	High	Medium
	Forecasts are obtained by smoothing, averaging, past actual values in a linear or exponential manner	Medium	High	Medium
Qualitative or Judgemental				
Salesforce estimate	A bottom-up approach aggregating salespersons' forecasts	Low	High	Low
Juries of executive opinions	Marketing, production and finance executives jointly prepare forecasts	Low	High	Low
Anticipatory surveys; market research	Learning about intentions of potential customers or plans of business	Medium	Medium	Medium
Scenario	Forecasters imagine the impacts of anticipated conditions	Low	Medium	Low
Delphi	Experts are guided towards a consensus	Low	Medium	Medium
Brainstorming	Idea generation in a non-critical group situation	Low	Medium	Medium

7 Accounting Applications
Mohamed Bayou

7.1 INTRODUCTION

Accounting is one of the major disciplines in which computer technology has had its largest applications. This is largely due to the quantitative nature of accounting; most of the accounting cycles, procedures, and models are classifiable into logical detailed steps where the transaction data are the inputs and the various accounting external and internal reports are the outputs. In addition, the size and diversity of these reports, some of which are required by law; the required degree of precision in the data; the timeliness of the reports; and the numerous different users of the accounting information are some of the factors which have made computer applications in this discipline not only favourable but also necessary.

With the numerous advantages of computers such as speed, precision, economy, and ability to handle a complex myriad volume of data, computer applications in accounting are increasingly demanded. The impact of the computer on the accounting profession is substantial; the volume of data that can be processed with the computer has a significant effect on the planning and control functions and on the reporting systems. Consequently, computers enhance accountants' productivity and effectiveness, hence providing them with opportunities to play greater roles in the business world and the society at large. However, computers create different opportunities for intentional and unintentional irregularities in handling assets and information. The security and control measures against the misuse and abuse of computers are challenging skills for the accountants. In addition, accountants are required to learn and be familiar with the various processing devices and packages available for use to gain insight into the potential benefits of computers (Endriga, 1982, p. 38). Inclusion of this requirement in the curricula of accounting programs of educational and vocational institutions in developing nations would enhance the computer skills and increase accounting applications in these countries.

This chapter discusses the general effects and applications of computer technology in the areas of financial accounting, managerial accounting, auditing and taxation. Finally, the major problems faced in a computerised environment, such as computer crimes and security, are addressed. Computer security has been a concern of managers in developing countries and it is commonly considered a reason, among others, for unwillingness to use computers.

7.2   APPLICATIONS IN FINANCIAL ACCOUNTING

The basic accounting cycle is the core of financial accounting since Luca Pacciolo ('the father of accounting' as he is usually called by accountants) wrote his book on the mechanism of the double entry system in 1494. The accounting cycle in a manual system, which is still used by many small and medium size organisations in developing countries, can be summarised as follows:

1. Journalising: The journal is often called the record of original entry. Transactions are recorded in the journal periodically by following the double entry system where each transaction has a debit side and a credit side. These transactions should be supported by documents such as sale or purchase slips or receipts, vouchers, checks, and bank statements before their recording in the journal.
2. Posting to the ledger: The ledger is a collection of accounts. These accounts include assets, liabilities, owners' equities, revenues and expenses. Posting means transferring the amounts of debits and credits in each journal entry to the specific accounts in the ledger affected by the transactions.
3. Preparing a trial balance: A trial balance is a method of checking the accuracy of journalising and posting to the ledger. It consists of two columns, one for the debit balances and the other for the credit balances. The total of the debit balances should equal the total of the credit balances, otherwise an error exists, and should be corrected before proceeding to the next step in the accounting cycle.
4. Preparing adjusting entries: Adjusting entries are made at the end of each fiscal period to account for all of the expenses and revenues of that period. For example, depreciation expense for using machinery and buildings is not incurred as a result of a business transaction. Nevertheless, the expense should be recorded (charged) by an adjusting entry at the end of the period in which the assets were used in operations.

5. A trial balance is usually made after journalising and posting the adjusting entries.
6. Preparing financial statements: The income statement, the balance sheet, and the statement of changes in financial position are prepared after step 5 above is completed. A worksheet with many columns is usually utilised for this purpose.
7. Preparing closing entries: 'Nominal' accounts such as expense and revenue accounts are closed to the general, 'Income Summary Account', so that the accounting books are ready for recording the activities of the following year.
8. A post-closing trial balance is usually prepared at the end of the accounting cycle. This trial balance includes only the 'real' accounts of assets, liabilities, and owners' equities.

This accounting cycle which is usually called 'book-keeping' is computerisable in its entirety. Business enterprises may have hundreds of accounts and transactions affecting these accounts. Hence, the computer capability is not comparable with the human one in this application. It should be noted that the contents of the journal and ledger are unreadable in their normal form in a computerised system since the contents are stored in discs or tapes. This non-visibility problem has some implications for auditors as will be discussed later.

Payroll

Payroll functions are almost impossible to handle without a computer in large and most medium-size companies. There are so many deductions to be made from the gross pay for each employee. In the USA, examples of these deductions are federal income tax, state income tax, county or city income tax, social security taxes on the employee, and many other voluntary deductions such as health and life insurance fees, professional or club dues, charity contributions, and other miscellaneous savings. Also, there are many taxes connected to the payroll and payable by the employer. These taxes and deductions have different rates, and copies of their statements should be supplied to different parties, including the government, the employee, and the accounting department. The importance of the computer in the payroll area cannot be overemphasised. The payroll deductions for a particular organisation or a country vary; however, the payroll process involves numerous deductions and renders the payroll function as an excellent area for computerisation in developing countries.

Disclosure

One of the major factors affecting accounting has been the trend toward more disclosure of information. An example of expanding disclosure is the requirement made by the Securities and Exchange Commission (SEC), a federal agency, and the Financial Accounting Standards Board (FASB) in the USA to report supplementary data based on constant dollar accounting and current cost accounting in addition to historical cost financial statements published by major corporations. The computer is of great assistance for accountants to meet this increasing demand for disclosure.

GAAP and EDP

Financial accounting is governed by a set of rules known as generally accepted accounting principles (GAAP). Computers are more efficient processors than humans in handling the business transactions data according to the GAAP especially if multiple purposes are sought, for example, evaluation of accounting policies and application of budgetary techniques (Will, 1980, pp. 171 and 172). The spreadsheet and the Oz, discussed below, are some of the software packages that can be useful in this direction. However, some tasks cannot be computerised. These tasks involve decision-making which requires human creativity, ingenuity, and intelligence (Will, 1980, p. 172). Thus, there is a need to distinguish between tasks that can be processed by machines, and tasks that can only be performed by humans. This may be accomplished through combining in a logical coherent framework the GAAP and general acceptability guidelines of the electronic data processing (EDP) system. For this purpose, the Committee for Modern Accounting Systems of the West German public profession published an opinion in 1975, 'On the Interpretation of Generally Accepted Accounting Principles with the Application of EDP Systems in Accounting' (Will, 1980, p. 179). The opinion established several criteria for acceptability of an EDP system including completeness, correctness, timeliness, security, and auditability (Will, 1980, p. 180). These criteria have the objective of establishing validity and acceptability of the system's output. In turn, acceptability of information enhances its utilisation and the quality of decisions.

Spreadsheets

An electronic spreadsheet is a form of worksheet with many rows and columns. The rows are identified by alphabetic characters (A to Z, AA to AZ, BA to BZ, etc.) The columns are numbered, e.g., 1 to 2048 in Lotus 1–2–3. Therefore, each cell in the spreadsheet is identified by its row letter and column number, e.g., A1, B35, Z752. A rectangular group of cells is called a 'range' and is identified by two cells, the cell on the upper-left corner, and the cell on the lower-right-hand corner. The cells can be filled with either labels (headings) or values by the user. Labels are entered by typing the desired alphabetic or other characters. Values are either numbers, mathematical symbols, or formulas. All arithmetic operations may be performed on values. Labels may only communicate information; any arithmetic operation attempted will find the label defined as a zero (Killough and Leininger, 1984, pp. 773–4).

A spreadsheet is available through a template where all labels and formulas have been entered, therefore, enabling a user to enter only his or her data. The spreadsheet templates are organised into four basic parts: (1) Information, instruction or label screen, (2) Input screen, (3) Output screen, and (4) Computations (Killough and Leininger, 1984, pp. 780 and 781).

The spreadsheet was invented by Dan Bricklin, a Harvard Business School student, and his programming friend, Robert Frankston in 1978. They formed a company named Software Arts to develop what became VisiCalc. Personal Software (now VisiCorp) was established to market the software. Many other firms entered this market such as Apple II, Sorcim Corporation's SuperCalc, Lotus Development Corporation, and IBM (Killough and Leininger, 1984, pp. 778 and 779).

Spreadsheets are becoming more popular among accountants for their simplicity and similarity to the typical accounting worksheet (Killough and Leininger, 1984, p. 773).

The Oz

The Oz, created by Fox and Geller, is considered an expansion of the electronic spreadsheet. The term 'Oz' is intended to indicate something magical, from the story 'The Wizard of Oz'. The Oz has the capability to hold several sets of information including actual data and budgeted and forecast data. In other words, the Oz's capability is equivalent to working with five spreadsheets simultaneously, allowing it probably to be the first of a new generation in professional and business software (Moody, 1984, p. 15).

7.3 APPLICATIONS IN MANAGERIAL ACCOUNTING

The trend in the information revolution is toward the creation of massive databases, not only nationally but also internationally. For example, the United Kingdom's Datastream Service developed for the City of London is now also used in Holland, Switzerland and Germany (Banyard, 1982, p. 34). Facilitating this trend are several broad technology changes. These include the availability of a wide range of inexpensive facilities with tremendous storage capacity; elimination of many telecommunication problems; recognition and familiarity with different processing devices and their potential benefits; and the progressive developments in computer technology to handle situations with imperfect information (Banyard, 1982, p. 33). These technological changes have substantial effects on managerial accounting. More information that can be handled in terms of quantity, quality, and speed of assimilation, has led to more comprehensive analysis and more effective control of operations. Organisations in both developed and developing countries have achieved a higher level of accounting generally, thereby creating a good basis for managerial accounting practices (Banyard, 1982, p. 32). These changes, however, have created a demand for acquiring knowledge and skill for effective utilisation of computers on the part of managerial accountants (Banyard, 1982). It follows that in order to be more effective and creative, managerial accountants in developing countries are required to keep up with computer changes not only in their own environments, but also with changes in developed countries. Specific managerial accounting applications are discussed below.

Managerial accounting is concerned with planning and control at responsibility centres. These responsibility centres are either cost centres (controlling costs only) such as maintenance and repair centre; profit centres (controlling revenues and costs) such as a branch in a department store; or investment centres (controlling revenues, costs, and investments) such as a division in a large corporation. To carry out the planning and control functions, details of data are needed. These details are feedback and feedforward information. Generally speaking, more details mean more opportunities for financial control (Northridge, 1980, p. 24). This detail aspect is referred to as micro-accounting (Northridge, 1980). Nowadays, this concept can be implemented relatively cheaply by many available systems such as microcomputers, minicomputers, and on-line systems (Northridge, 1980, p. 25).

Budgeting is part of the planning function. There are many types of budgets, for example, the master budget, the flexible budget, and the zero-base budget. Sensitivity analysis is very important to develop an acceptable and realistic budget. For example, in the master budget where all of the functional budgets such as the production budget, the raw materials budget, the labor budget, and the cash budget are typically based on the sales budget. Sensitivity analysis usually raises questions such as, 'What will be the net income if the advertising budget is increased by one million dollars? By two million dollars? etc'. This type of 'what-if?' question can be raised about any other critical resource such as labour or machinery. Changing any variable or forecast in the budget structure may affect all of the individual budgets down to the budgeted financial statements. Sensitivity analysis, i.e., plugging different forecasts into the budget system is necessary to come up with the acceptable blend of realistic forecasts and attainable management goals. Computer devices such as the spreadsheet and the Oz, discussed earlier, are helpful tools for carrying out numerous iterations of sensitivity analysis.

The control function partially depends on comparing the budgeted results with the actual results, i.e., on variance analysis. The deviation between the budgeted result and the actual result is called a variance. In the traditional variance analysis, there are two variances for every resource: A price variance and a quantity (or efficiency) variance. For example, direct raw materials have the following two variances:

Direct Raw Material Price Variance = Actual quantity purchased (actual price paid per unit − Standard or budgeted price to be paid per unit)
Direct Raw Material Quantity Or Efficiency Variance = Standard price to be paid per unit (actual quantity used in production − standard quantity that should have been used in production).

To illustrate, a manufacturing company purchased and used 1000 lbs of raw materials in production. The price expected or budgeted to be paid is $5 per pound. However, the actual price paid was $6. Actual production was 250 finished units. According to the engineers of the company, each unit of output should take not more than 3 lbs. The raw material variances are computed as follows:

Direct Raw Material Price Variance = 1000 lbs ($6 − $5) = $1000 unfavourable

Direct Raw Material Efficiency Variance = $5 (1000 lbs − (250 units × 3 lbs)) = $5 (1000 lbs − 750 lbs) = $1250 favourable.

A possible explanation for these variances as shown on the performance report may be that the purchasing department paid a higher price for a better quality of raw materials (hence the unfavourable price variance of $1000). The better quality materials lead to savings in the use of materials in production (thus the favourable efficiency variance of $1250). The overall result is a net favourable variance of $250 ($1250 favourable minus $1000 unfavourable) which indicates a good performance. The reader can imagine many other reasons for these variances.

There can be many variances since there are many types of raw materials, different labour skills, and numerous manufacturing overhead items. The micro-accounting concept discussed above is applicable to this subject.

Variances are considered exceptions and this is the core of the 'management by exception' concept. That is, since managerial time is valuable, a manager's attention should be directed only to the deviation of actual performance from the budgets or plans. The scarce resource of managerial time should not be wasted on areas where actual performance is in harmony with the plans. However, not all variances are considered exceptions in need of prompt management attention. There are at least four criteria for a variance to be described as an exception:

1. *Materiality* For example, consider only variances which are $10 000 or 10 per cent of the budgeted amount whichever is lower.
2. *Controllability* Some variances are beyond management control, e.g., a purchasing manager may not be able to control the raw material price variance. Prices are usually a result of market conditions over which the manager has no control. Hence, this variance does not need too much management attention.
3. *Type* For example, investigate all variances in cash, no matter how small, if fraud is suspected.

4. *Consistency* If a variance is constantly favourable (i.e., actual result is less than the budget) this may indicate that the standard or the budget is too relaxed or not stringent enough. Thus, the standard or budget should be adjusted to promote more efficiency in the use of resources.

Some of these criteria can be computerised. Therefore, a computer signal can direct management attention to where it is needed, thus facilitating the control function.

Another aspect of variance analysis arises from the fact that control is a short-term concept. That is, variances should be reported as soon as possible so that correction of the areas deviating from the preset plans can be made in time. For example, an unfavourable raw material efficiency variance may indicate that the cutting machine wastes so much raw material that it needs to be repaired or replaced. The sooner this variance is reported the more control can be placed over materials waste.

In summary, variances are numerous; they have certain criteria to warrant management time and attention; and should be reported as soon as possible. These three factors make computer application to this area very important.

Another computer application is in linear programming technique. Consider the example in Table 7.1.

Table 7.1 *Partial income statement on per-unit basis*

| | Products | |
	A	*B*
Sale price per unit	$10	$15
Variable cost per unit	4	7
Contribution margin per unit	$ 6	$ 8

If only one product is to be produced, then it should be B, since its contribution margin, $8, is higher. However, if more information is added in this example, the decision will change. Suppose that only 1000 machine hours are available and 2 units of product A can be produced in one machine hour and only one unit of product B can be produced in one machine hour. Which product should be produced? The answer is product A. Machine hours are the scarce resource. In one machine hour, $12 of contribution margin will result if product A is produced and only $8 contribution margin will result if product B is produced. Hence, total contribution margin is $12 000 (i.e., $12 times 1000 machine hours) if A is produced and only $8000 (i.e., $8 times 1000 machine hours) will result if B is produced. Obviously, product A is more profitable to produce. In this example, only one scarce resource is assumed. In real life, there can be several scarce resources in terms of types of raw material, different skills of labour, different overhead items, storage space available, limitations on production volume due to government restrictions, etc. In a case with many scarce resources or constraints, a linear programming model is more appropriate. However, a feasible solution to the model may not be obtained unless a computer program is applied. Fortunately, there are many linear programming packages available at reasonable prices.

In the area of inventory controls, there are many models, e.g., the economic order quantity (EOQ), the reorder point, and the ABC method. These models can be handled totally by a computer. For example, a computer can be programmed to signal out when to order, and how much to order. With the aid of computers, different probabilities and different states of nature (e.g., optimistic, most likely, and pessimistic) can be incorporated to handle problems of stockouts and overstocking of raw materials and goods. Thus, these inventory models can be made more sophisticated and useful for managerial decisions.

Other computer applications are in the areas of cost-volume-profit analysis where sensitivity analysis is important; in regression analysis; and in process costing where different resources are introduced at different stages, different batches or jobs are at different stages of completion, and costing of these jobs is needed for financial accounting purposes and for managerial accounting purposes. This is by no means an exhaustive list of computer applications in managerial accounting.

It should be noted that managerial accounting is probably the most important branch of the accounting discipline in developing countries. Managerial accounting is concerned with efficiency and effectiveness; efficiency is the relationship between inputs and outputs and effectiveness is the relationship of the results to the goals of the organisation. Many of the developing countries depend for their income on one or two natural resources such as oil, phosphate, and forestry. These resources are of exhaustive values; they are irreplaceable. Hence, in developing nations, the efficiency and effectiveness notions are vital for decisions concerned with optimum allocation of scarce resources and the building of sound economic development programs.

7.4 COMPUTER APPLICATIONS IN AUDITING

A comprehensive definition of an audit considers it as being 'a methodical review and objective examination, both of which include the process of verifying specific information as determined by the auditor or as established by general practice. Generally, the purpose of an audit is the expression of an opinion or conclusion about that which was audited' (Miller and Bailey, 1984, p. 1.01). Mautz and Sharaf listed five primary auditing concepts: (1) Evidence, (2) Due audit care, (3) Fair presentation, (4) Independence of the auditor, and (5) Ethical conduct (Mautz and Sharaf, 1961).

This indicates that, in large part, the audit process is labour-intensive and judgemental. Consequently, computer audit techniques are mainly applied to some audit manual methods rather than the computerisation of the entire audit process (Vasarhelyi, 1983, p. 32). This may explain why the public accounting profession has been slow in adopting new computer technologies. For example, even though in 1968 there were approximately 25 000 general purpose computer systems installed in the USA, little was published on the effect of computers on the audit process or on audit procedures that fit a highly automated environment (Richardson, 1983). A general conclusion of the literature written in early 1960s on auditing EDP systems was that the auditor of computerised accounting systems needs a minimal knowledge of EDP (Cerullo, 1978, p. 67). However, during that era it was felt that computers would play a major role in the future to the point that 'the computer and the auditor will be partners. There will never be any reason for the auditor to become subservient to non-human equipment, although he may become subservient to or even be replaced by another auditor who understands computers' (Carlson, 1967, p. 314).

An interesting development in the 1970s is the emergence of a new group consisting of technical computer audit experts. These experts who are either employees in or consultants for large accounting firms, have assisted in speeding up computer applications in auditing. However, they may have allowed other professionals in these firms to pay less attention to acquiring computer skills. This is expected to change in the near future since many accountants are now graduating from many educational and vocational institutions with some knowledge of computer technologies. Thus, the role of the technical computer audit experts may not only change materially, but also they may cease to exist as a separate group (List, 1983, p. 53). It is expected that as computers become more flexible, more reliable, less time-consuming, and less expensive and as opportunities to acquire computer skills are increasing, accountants will be less intimidated by computers and more eager to learn the technology. As late entrants into the computerised accounting field, developing countries can gain this advantage in training their accountants.

In the following paragraphs, more specific applications are discussed.

Evaluation of internal control

The American Institute of Certified Public Accountants (AICPA) defines internal control as follows: 'Internal control comprises the plan of organization and all of the coordinate methods and measures adopted within a business to safequard its assets, check the accuracy and reliability of its accounting data, promote operational efficiency, and encourage adherence to prescribed managerial policies' (Statement on Auditing Procedures No. 33, 1963, pp. 27 and 28). The external auditor is required to evaluate the internal control system in charge of his or her engagement. First, the system is evaluated in terms of the adequacy of its procedures and their combinations. The combination of procedures may involve a large number of variations which are better evaluated by electronic data processing (Vasarhelyi, 1983, p. 35). Second, compliance testing is conducted to assess the adequacy of the system. This is done through the sampling technique which may lead to larger or smaller substantive samples (Vasarhelyi, 1983, p. 35).

Audit planning and staff assignment

In large auditing firms, there is a need for scheduling the audit process into a set of steps. There can be numerous different sets of steps. A network model may be applied to find the optimal set (route) that satisfies the firm's policies concerning protection against possible liability claims, cost of the audit engagement, etc. In addition, the staff members may be assigned to the audit processes on a long-term or short-term basis. The Linear programming and a microcomputer spreadsheet software may be utilised to find the optimal assignment with the firm's policies and characteristics (seniority, experience, specialisation, etc.) of auditors as constraints (Vasarhelyi, 1983, pp. 34 and 35).

Finally, word processors may be utilised in auditing to prepare many standardized documents such as audit bid proposals, engagement letters, contracts and confirmations (Vasarhelyi, 1983, p. 34). Financial accounting databases such as COMPUSTAT and Value Line may be utilised to conduct financial analysis comparing the firm being audited and other firms in the same industry and other industries (Vasarhelyi, 1983, p. 34). In short, computer applications in auditing are increasingly adopted especially in the developed countries. However, we should remember Mathieson's caution that 'computer assisted techniques do not take the place of other audit tests of the [accounting] system; they are part of the total evaluation process' (Mathieson, 1979, p. 12).

7.5 APPLICATIONS IN TAXATIONS

In many countries, the tax laws are complex. This is due to the different objectives of tax regulations and frequent changes in these regulations. The calculations of taxable income are usually difficult because of the many exclusions, deductions, credits, and different methods that should be employed. Added to the problem of tax complexities is the time pressure of the tax season, which is a comparatively short but intense period filled with critical deadlines regarding payroll reporting, year-end closing, audit reports, etc. (Schneidman, 1983, p. 57). Computers can be helpful in this area due to their tremendous speed and storage capability. However, it is thought that, 'the taxation area is least affected by electronic computer systems' (Cerullo, 1978, p. 69). The reason is probably related to the judgemental nature of tax planning; a professional judgement or decision is needed in complex tax situations. This may explain why most computer generated tax returns are prepared by specialised service bureaus. Instead, a taxpayer may prepare his tax returns by himself, i.e., in-house preparation. In-house preparations are on the rise as accountants are becoming more familiar with computer technology. The time and cost per return of the in-house preparation may be lower (Heinemann, 1981, p. 15). Therefore, the accountant will prepare his tax returns on his computer when he can not cost-justify the service bureau preparation (Schneidman, 1983, p. 57).

Private and public accountants specialising in taxation should be familiar with the various packaged programs offered by many services for preparing tax returns and tax planning. For example, time-shared computer programs are available in the USA through service bureaus and through General Electric Company's time-sharing network to AICPA members (Cerullo, 1978, p. 69).

In many developing countries, the tax system is not complicated. For example, in most oil producing countries such as Saudi Arabia, Kuwait, and Libya, the individual income tax liability is virtually zero for a large segment of the population. The corollary of this situation is that in these countries, computerising the tax systems is of a lower priority in comparison with other computer applications.

7.6 MAJOR PROBLEMS INVOLVED IN COMPUTER APPLICATIONS

Computer technology has brought with it several problems for the accounting profession. Some of the major problems, which the accountant in a developing country seeking to use computers should be aware of, are discussed in the following:

1. The trend in the 1960s and 1970s was towards centralisation of data processing due to the substantial economies of scale that could be derived from acquisition of large computer systems (Lee and Wilkins, 1983, p. 29). That is, centralised systems may permit an organisation to develop a common data base which reduces expensive redundancy in record keeping (Lee and Wilkins, 1983, p. 29). However, the centralisation or integration of accounting data systems has several impacts. For example, the condition of effective segregation of responsibilities for the internal control system is difficult to maintain. This condition requires that no one person should be assigned unsupervised access to parts of the system that allow him or her to commit an error or enter fraudulent data, and then to cancel the error or fraud without detection. In a computerised environment, the duties that should be the responsibilities of different persons are

those relating to the computer library; system development and programming; hardware operations; and performance measurement.

2. The records of the manual accounting cycle have changed and some of these records are eliminated. For example, the data accumulated in the ledger in a manual system are stored in machine-readable files such as magnetic tapes or disks. These are not readable in their natural state. The importance of the journal as the mainstream of processing decreases in an EDP system if significant items are produced for reporting purposes on an exception basis (Porter and Perry 1981, p. 7). In general, accounting books have become electronic files of different designs (Will, 1980, p. 169).

3. The control function in a manual system is largely performed by individuals. In a computerised system, this function is shifted to the computer via edit routines including program checks to ensure the accuracy, completeness, and reasonableness of input flows through the system (Porter and Perry, 1981, p. 8). Edit routines are systematic procedures (instructions) which inspect and accept or reject transaction inputs according to validity or reasonableness of quantity, amounts, codes, and other data. Thus, errors or irregularities in data input can be detected upon their being entered into the computer (Porter and Perry, 1981, p. 98).

4. The audit trail, consisting of tracing the data through documents, journals, ledgers, and worksheets, to validate the information reported in financial statements, is different in an EDP system. For example, the development of data collection equipment, communication facilities, and random-access memories eliminates or reduces the need for maintaining source documents (Porter and Perry, 1981, p. 7). Furthermore, machines that accept voice communication are currently available on the market. This enables the accountant to make journal entries by speaking to the machine without any supporting documentation (List, 1983, p. 52). Documents or vouchers are usually required by law to support accounting entries and the occurrence of bonafide transactions. The Committee for Modern Accounting Systems of West Germany in 1975 viewed that, 'Insofar as the law prescribes a visual representation of the vouchers, storage of their contents on data storage media alone does not meet the voucher function' (Will, 1980, p. 181).

5. Computer technology has created new types of risk; these are due to potential losses from unintentional and intentional errors.

Unintentional errors are caused by the misuse of hardware, software, input and output data. Auditors are constantly required to improve their 'auditing through the computer and around the computer' techniques to detect or eliminate these errors in order to keep pace with new developments in computer technology.

Intentional errors are commonly termed 'computer crime'. Indeed, the computer has created opportunities for crime that have never been available before (Campitelli, 1983, p. 46). A new class of criminals has emerged that endangers controls over resources and protection of classified information (Endriga, 1982, p. 45). The normal crime prevention and detection techniques are helpless in this respect because usually there are no fingerprints left on the hardware, there are no tell-tale signs of computer file or program manipulation, and the criminal does not have to be in the computer room or even in the building (Campitelli, 1983, p. 46). With sophisticated computer equipment currently available, access to the computer is only a telephone call away (Campitelli, 1983, p. 46). As a result, computer crimes increased substantially. In the USA, studies conducted by the FBI revealed that computer fraud rises by 500 per cent each year where the average loss per crime is approximately $500 000, and only about one per cent of these crimes are actually detected (Endriga, 1982, p. 45). One of the well-known computer crime cases in the USA is the Equity Funding Corporation fraud involving $2 billion embezzlement (Porter and Perry, 1981, p. 8).

Other studies showed that computer frauds account for between two and five per cent of the GNP of most industrialised countries (Endriga, 1982, p. 45). Meanwhile, losses to banks from fraud are 500 per cent greater than losses from violence or robbery (Endriga, 1982, p. 45). Other dangers due to the misuse of computers are the invasion of privacy, the manipulation of recorded facts in many profit-oriented and nonprofit-oriented organisations, and even the possibility of involving the super powers in a third world war. However, so far, the business sector appears to be the one which suffered most from computer misuse (Endriga, 1982, p. 45).

6. Because of the problems discussed in (5) above, discussion of security in the computerised environment began to appear extensively in the literature recently. In general, security measures are designed to reduce risk. There are several sources (exposures) of risk. Mair, Wood, and Davis (1978 p. 11.) discussed the concepts of 'exposures', 'cause of exposure', and 'control'. They listed nine types of exposures:

Erroneous record keeping
Unacceptable accounting

Business interruption
Erroneous management decisions
Fraud and embezzlement
Statutory sanctions
Excessive costs/deficient revenues
Loss or destruction of assets
Competitive disadvantages

While these exposures are not mutually exclusive, they do not arise simply due to lack of controls. They are caused; therefore, causes must exist before exposures result. In turn, a control acts to eliminate or reduce a cause of exposure rather than directly affecting the exposure (Mair, Wood, and Davis, 1978, pp. 12 and 13). Notice that one control technique may affect several causes, while one specific cause may be controlled by various control techniques. An exposure is measured by the effect of a cause stated in money terms multiplied by the probability of its occurrence (Mair, Wood, and Davis, 1978, p. 13). The resulting figure is to be compared with an acceptable level of risk (Bund, 1975, pp. 149 and 150). This acceptable level of risk may differ from firm to firm and even from one management level to another within the same firm. Generally, the 'cost' of any control technique adopted should be compared to its 'benefits' as measured by the resulting reduction in the amount of exposure (Bund, 1975, p. 150). Installation of the control technique is justified when the estimated benefits exceed the costs.

The exposures listed above exist in a manual as well as in a computerised system. The use of computers does not change the nature of these exposures. However, it changes the nature and frequency of the causes of exposures. Hence, different controls must be adopted in a computerised system to eliminate or reduce the causes.

In his discussion of computer security, Wilkes emphasised the distinction between security management and protection for all security systems regardless of being manual or computerised. That is, security management refers to the authorised access to the computer, while protection refers to the authorised use of the contents of the computerised information once access to the computer is granted to the user. In this sense, 'protection' will prevent the user from copying information from one file with certain security classification to another file with lower level of classification directly or after manipulation (Wilkes, 1984, p. 3). This procedure is called 'confinement' (Wilkes, 1984, p. 3). Several approaches or models appear in the literature to increase the capabilities (or domain) of protection. However, some of these models have the effect of increasing the complexities of software (Wilkes, 1984, p. 6).

In any event, the control techniques intended to increase the security of a computerised system should include more than the services of internal and external auditors and the installation of protective devices. Probably the most valuable ingredient to increase security is the integrity of individuals who have access to the system. Whenever the integrity of the individuals becomes questionable, and perhaps this is becoming normal in an era of rising white-collar crime, the carrying of fidelity bonds by the employer becomes a necessity.

7.   From the above discussion, the cost of a computerised system includes more than the purchase price of the hardware and software and other facilities. It also includes the cost of the security system and losses from the residual risk not covered by the security system. Expanding the security system to cover the potential losses of the residual risk is assumed to be unjustifiable by cost-benefit analysis. These latter losses are typically treated as ordinary business expenses just like the treatment of the losses from uncollectable customer debts. The cost of the hardware and the security system are normally capitalised and charged to income over the period of their useful lives. However, a controversy exists regarding the accounting for software. Should the cost of software be amortised or depreciated separately from the cost of the hardware equipment? Is a software package a tangible or an intangible asset? In the USA, the Internal Revenue Service asserted that computer software is an intangible asset; therefore, the owner is prevented from using accelerated depreciation methods or taking advantage of the investment tax credit. Hence, the federal income tax increases. However, treating the software as an intangible asset decreases the bases for computing property, sales, and use taxes. These taxes are a source of revenue for the states. The loss of potential revenues due to the intangible treatment of software lead most states to treat the software as a tangible asset (Raabe, 1984, p. 227). This inconsistency of treatment between the federal and state governments leads to many court cases and the issue is still unresolved (Raabe, 1984, p. 227). Other countries may benefit from the American experience relating to the tangible/intangible classification of software assets.

Computer software – whether operational software or applicational software – is a set of written instructions. These instructions *per se* are intangible. However, the hardware is helpless (can not operate or function) without these instructions. In other words, the software does not only expand the utility of hardware, it is also a part of it. That is, the hardware and software are two components of one entity, the computer system. The author is of the opinion that the reasonable cost of software packages intended to be used with the hardware equipment should be added to the cost of the hardware (tangible) asset and accounted for as one asset. The cost of software is necessary to have the tangible asset ready for normal use. This necessity is the criteria adopted in accounting theory to capitalise sales tax, transportation cost, and installation cost as part of the cost of a purchased fixed asset. These costs are intangible, but they are capitalised and depreciated along with the purchase price of the related fixed asset.

In conclusion, computer technology can be of great assistance to developing countries' accounting professions. The computer can speed up the learning process for these countries, enabling them to catch up with the advanced practices of industrialized nations, and avoid several of their problems. Furthermore, computers may help to harmonise the accounting standards of different countries and promote international accounting as an international language.

References

AICPA Committee on Auditing Procedures, (1963) *Statement on Auditing Procedures No. 33, Auditing standards and Procedures*, (New York: AICPA).

BANYARD, CYRIL (1982) 'Computer Technology and Its Effects on Management Accounting', *Management Accounting*, September, pp. 32–35.

BUND, MELVIN (1975) 'Security in an Electronic Data Processing Environment', *The Accountants Digest*, March, pp. 149–151.

CAMPITELLI, VINCENT A. (1983) 'Computer Crime – A Growing Problem. Is There A Solution?', *The Accounting Forum*, (December 1982-January 1983), pp. 45–50.

CARLSON, ARTHUR E. (1967) 'Automation and the Future of Accounting', *The Accounting Sampler, An Introduction*, Thomas J. Burns and Harvey S. Hendrickson, (eds.) (New York: McGraw-Hill Book Company), pp. 312–316.

CERULLO, MICHAEL J. (1978) 'Computer Knowledge and Expertise of Public Accountants', *The Accountants Digest*, December, pp. 67–71.

ENDRIGA, BALTAZAR N. (1982) 'The Impact of Computers on the ASEAN Accounting Profession', *Accountants' Journal*, (published by

Philippine Institute of Certified Public Accountants), First Semester, pp. 37–49.

HEINEMANN, H. PETER (1981) 'Computerizing the Public Practice', *The Accountants Digest*, September, pp. 13–17.

KILLOUGH, LARRY N. and WAYNE E. LEININGER (1984) *Cost Accounting, Concepts and Techniques for Management*, (St. Paul, Mn.: West Publishing Co.).

LEE, SANG M. and SUSAN J. WILKINS (1983) 'Computer Facility Centralization/Decentralization: A Multiobjective Analysis Model', *An International Journal, Computers and Operations Research*, Volume 1, No. 1, pp. 29–40.

LIST, WILLIAM (1983) 'How Cheap Computers are Affecting External Audit', *The Accountant's Magazine*, February, pp. 52–54.

MAIR, WILLIAM C.; DONALD R. WOOD; and KEAGLE W. DAVIS (1978) *Computer Control And Audit*, (Altamonte, FL: The Institute of Internal Auditors).

MATHIESON, ROBERT (1979) 'Computer Assisted Audit Techniques', *The Accountants Digest*, September, pp. 11–14.

MAUTZ, R. K. and HUSSEIN A. SHARAF (1961) *The Philosophy of Auditing*, (Chicago: American Accounting Association).

MILLER, MARTIN A. and LARRY P. BAILEY (1984) *Miller's Comprehensive GAAS Guide*, (San Diego, Cal.: Miller Accounting Publications, Inc.).

MOODY, GLYN (1984) 'Beyond the Spreadsheet?', *The Accountant*, 22 March, pp. 15–16.

NEWMAN, CHARLES (1984) 'Low Cost Accounting Packages III – Graffcom', *The Accountant*, 26 April, pp. 15–16.

NORTHRIDGE, ROYSTON L. (1980) 'Micro-Accounting in a Micro Age', *Management Accounting*, January, pp. 24–25.

PORTER, W. THOMAS and WILLIAM E. PERRY (1981) *EDP, Controls and Auditing*, third edition, (Boston: Kent Publishing Company).

RAABE, WILLIAM A. (1984) 'Property, Sales, and Use Taxation of Custom and "Canned" Computer Software: Emerging Judicial Guidelines', *The Tax Executive*, April, pp. 227–237.

RICHARDSON, DANA R. (1983) 'The Impact of Technology on Auditing', *The Accounting Forum*, (December 1982–January 1983), pp. 14–29.

SCHNEIDMAN, ARNOLD (1983) 'The Impact of the Computer on the Accounting Profession', *The Accounting Forum*, (December 1982–January 1983), pp. 51–59.

VASARHELYI, MIKLOS A. (1983) 'A Framework for Audit Automation: Online Technology and the Audit Process', *The Accounting Forum*, (December 1982–January 1983), pp. 30–44.

WILL, HARTMUT J. (1980) 'Computerized Accounting: International Issues', *The International Journal of Accounting*, Fall, pp. 169–207.

WILKES, MAURICE V. (1984) 'Security management and Protection – A Personal Approach', *The Computer Journal*, (a publication of The British Computer Society), February, pp. 3–7.

8 Computer Applications in Service Industries

O. Geoffrey Okogbaa

8.1 INTRODUCTION

In the developed nations, a general trend of the past few decades has been the continued improvement in the technology of production especially in manufacturing and other related activities. Advances in automation, especially in the production and processing of goods have enabled the increased demand for manufactured items to be met by a smaller proportion of the work force. The continued technological advancements in computers in particular and electronics in general, and the enhanced utilisation of automated work systems have led to a shift in employment from manufacturing to service organisations.

In the United States, as in most advanced economies, employment in the goods-producing industries rose only 9 percent between 1965 and 1968. In 1980, the total manufacturing labour force numbered about 23 million, which is about 22 per cent of the labour force. Significant gains in productivity resulting from automated production, improved machinery and technological breakthroughs permitted large increases in output without additional workers. Between 1978 and 1990, employment in goods-producing industries is expected to rise only from 28.7 million to 32.5 million for a growth of 13 per cent. (USBLS, 1980; 1981)

However, growth rates for white collar or knowledge worker occupations – professional, technical and management jobs – have increased. Once a small proportion of the labour force, knowledge workers now represent about half the total. The numbers of workers in service organisations have risen rapidly while those for blue collar workers have grown only slowly. Professionals and technical workers will grow from 14.2 million in 1978 to 16.9 million in 1990. Managers and administrators will grow from 10.1 million to 12.2 million in the same period. Much of the growth in professional, technical and knowledge worker employment has resulted from the growth of the service sector.

The continued growth of employment in the service sector is very definite. Most observers believe that the shift to the service sector will continue even if the actual growth rate is slow. With the current trend it is apparent that as the demand for services continue to increase, more attention will be focused on the application of available technology, especially computer technology in the service areas. Currently in the developing nations, computer applications in the service occupations include such areas as transportation, communication, banking and finance, education, health care and government. As their potential begins to be realised, often new services tend to arise. In addition, such procedures as billing and accounting have been routinised through computerisation and so have airline and hotel reservations.

The Bureau of Labor Statistics in the United States and the International Labor Office (ILO) have studied a number of white collar occupations in relation to computerisation and have arrived at the following results: (Hoos, 1960; USBLS, 1980; USBLS, 1981; Walker, 1967)

Communications Industry   Clerical employment is being reduced while professional and semi-professional employment, engineers, programmers, analysts will continue to grow.

Banking Industry   Employment is expected to continue to increase but at a decreasing rate. Bookkeepers are hardest hit by automation. The number of supervisory personnel has been growing. The introduction of automation has modified old jobs and created new ones. The principal new occupations are EDP (Electronic Data Processing) equipment operator, programmer, systems analyst, encoder and EDP clerk.

Insurance Carriers   Insurance carriers' employment will continue to grow slowly in the next few years.

Government   Employment is expected to continue to rise but only moderately. Professional and technical workers are expected to increase significantly.

For the developing economies, the expansion of the service sector is important for yet another reason. The government, and service-oriented industries, have always been responsible for the employment of a larger proportion of the work force in the developing nations. In some of the developing economies, the government employs about 70 per cent of the work force. (Taviss, 1970) And since most of the manufactured goods in these countries are imported, it stands to reason that a majority of the workers would be engaged in jobs or assignments that are service-oriented.

While without question the growth rates for the service occupations are different for the advanced economies *vis-à-vis* the developing nations, the trend in growth has remained the same. In other words, even though the magnitudes of the rates are grossly dissimilar for both economies, factors such as world trade and the mechanisms of the transfer of technology have enabled the acquisition of high levels of technology by the developing economies, thus making the trend somewhat similar.

8.2 AUTOMATION AND THE DEVELOPING NATIONS

Clearly, in the developed economies, computer technology has led to the availability of relevant and precise information on a more timely basis. To obtain such information requires the collection of current and accurate data. The pooling of such data and resources from various units of an organisation is necessary in order to provide a comprehensive database. The sharing of an information file will, among other things, reduce costly duplications. However, as is the case with most developing economies, such action is rendered ineffective by the very nature of the third world nation and by a number of factors, some of which are examined subsequently.

Factors that undermine information system development

Vested interest

Vested interest is characterised by fears, justifiable or otherwise, that the authority of the organisation or function in question is being diminished. Vested interests also enhance parochialism which tends to inhibit integration across the various levels of the organisation, especially where there is a decided need for organisational change. In the developing nations, this problem is very real. The disturbing aspect of it is that the fear that the authority or function of the organisation is being usurped or diminished is justified. Consequently it is not uncommon to find well orchestrated but subtle efforts designed to sabotage a program – however well meaning it may be.

Resistance to change

Resistance to change is a limiting factor of response to new ideas and technologies. It is the fear that change might upset the status quo, thereby diminishing spheres of influence. Resistance to change is not a developing nation phenomenon. However, it is amplified in these nations for obvious reasons. The development of a centralised data base means that information about individuals will be obtained very readily. In the developing countries, the concern is not only the invasion of privacy but how the information will ultimately be used. The state of affairs in the developing nations requires serious deliberation to determine a meaningful level and degree of centralisation.

Other factors

In addition to the aforementioned problems, there are some aspects of the culture and/or ethic of most developing nations which run contrary to some of the techniques and methodologies applicable to computer technology. Systems design and analysis, for instance, is a technique which depends very much on accurate data and clearly defined goals. In this technique a long-range goal is normally formulated, criteria developed and calculations made to identify which parts of the overall program do work and whether stated objectives are being achieved. The realities of the third world nations, however, often dictates a focus on more short-range objectives. In addition, there is the tendency on the part of the government agencies to withhold and sometimes 'massage' information that does not speak well of the agency's performance. This will ultimately affect the quality of data (Damachi, 1970; Fite, 1965; Sagasti, 1974).

8.3 NEED FOR COMPUTERISATION

Today, one of the operating philosophies of production in the advanced economies is 'work smarter, not harder'. This is the idea of putting to work the forces of nature that have been harnessed by science and technology. The opponents of the same philosophy for the developing nations argue that since the prevailing practices in these countries are far less sophisticated than those in use in the advanced economies, such practices or efforts must necessarily be carried on at a relatively elementary level of concept. The thrust of this argument is based on the axiom that 'you have to walk before you can run'. In other words, before government agencies or private businesses in the developing economies can be operated by the advanced methods used in the developing nations, they must necessarily repeat the stages of manual and/or simple mechanical methods which characterised the evolution of management practices in the developed countries.

The foregoing argument would be tenable if there were no mechanisms in existence for the transfer of appropriate technology, in which case it would make sense to repeat the onerous process of trial-and-error learning. However, the nature of world trade and technical cooperation are such that most available technologies can be acquired with little difficulty. In addition, the bulk of middle and top management personnel in these countries received their training in the developed nations and it is not far-fetched to expect that in their working lifetimes the processes of their government and business will be mechanised and automated. Thus, it is not clear that a lot will be gained by going through the manual and simple mechanical way of doing things especially if a way could be found to enable these countries to 'jump' immediately to the stages at which tasks are automated the same way they would be in a developed country under a comparable situation (Lynch and Rice, 1977; Taviss, 1970). Furthermore, it is the general consensus that the poor shape in which the economies of most developing nations find themselves is due to very low productivity. Consequently significant improvements in the economy could be achieved with modest gains in productivity. However, such manual and labour-intensive methods will not enhance output.

While the intent here is not to suggest that automation through computerisation will cure all the ills of the developing nations, it is fair to say that these nations would obtain the same advantages of economy, accuracy, speed, superior management information, and productivity, all of which have been the incentives for automation in those economies where advanced data processing methods are currently in use.

For the developing nations, there is perhaps a more meaningful gain from automation which may not be as significant for the advanced economies. This gain accrues from the conservation of scarce skills. Automation would help stretch the limited human resources further than any traditional method.

In the developing countries, computerisation will find its greatest use in the service industries since most manufactured items are imported and the bulk of the work force is employed in these industries.

8.4   COMPUTER APPLICATION

Before embarking on the investigation of possible computer applications in the service industries for developing nations, it is vital to establish some of the criteria that would establish the choice of jobs as possible candidates for computerization (Taviss, 1970). In the developed nations, the factors that may influence this choice include:

To gain economy

If the objective is economy (which is the case in most situations) and it is more work to prepare the data than it is to do the computation, then it is not meant for the computer. However, if the job or a significant part of it is highly repetitive, then it is suited for the computer.

To gain insight into a problem

If the computation will provide insight into a process such as a simulation process, then the computer is very well suited for such assignments. Simulations are used to investigate the behaviour of a model with real or assumed data before the real model is operational.

To gain job feasibility

Many jobs are possible only with the aid of computers, especially in situations where the results must be made available a very short period after the input has been initiated. The turn-round time required for the use of result is so small that it is impossible for humans to accomplish the needed computation within the time available.

On the whole, the moral about the suitability of a job for computer application is that if the decisions arising from the job assignments can be programmed, then the task is suited for computerisation. If the decision cannot be programmed, then it is probably not well suited for such applications. Decisions are programmed to the extent that a definite procedure has been worked out for handling them so that they do not have to be reworked or re-solved each time they occur. On the other hand, decisions are nonprogrammed to the extent that they are novel, unstructured and consequential. In non-programmed decisions there is no cut-and-dried approach for solving a problem since it has not been previously encountered or because its nature and/or structure is highly complex.

8.5 AREAS OF COMPUTER APPLICATION

Banking

Other than the government and its agencies, the commercial banks are about the largest processors of paperwork. In the developed countries, recording and reporting of operations of banks have developed and evolved over the years from one of manual processing of transactions through diverse stages of machine accounting to the present use of electronic computers for data processing.

The computer has affected banking operations in the developed nations in diverse ways. It has affected the internal structure and activities of the banking operations. It has made possible a variety of new customer services, and promises to play a vital role in the operations of a bank through its use in management information and decision support systems. It has altered the types, numbers and job assignments of bank personnel. In checking account and bookkeeping alone, the computer has supplanted some twenty individual manual procedures (Colton and Kramer, 1968). These operational changes have in turn caused changes in the form and extent of some of the traditional banking services.

In a few developing nations, there exist some limited computer applications in a number of banking operations. However, the level of application is miniscule when compared to the available computer technology and the degree of application in the developed nations. Currently in some of these nations, most banks open for business at 9 a.m. and close at 3 p.m. This is to enable the day's transactions to be recorded and updated before the next business day. It is not unusual to find bank employees leaving their offices at about 6 p.m. and on a very busy day (end of the month for example), this could even be much later. It is not uncommon to spend four to five hours and sometimes days trying to purchase traveller's cheques. The same can be said of most banking services. The reason for the long and sometimes protracted transaction times is that the transactions are manually processed. In addition, communications with branch offices can be a long process and may take hours or even days. It is thus apparent that automation, however modest, will have a significant impact on banking operations in most developing nations. Some of the banking services that if computerised hold great promise with regard to productivity improvement will include:

Demand deposit accounting

Demand deposit accounts are those accounts which the customer can access whenever desired, in other words, on demand. For this type of application in a developed country, a computer system with a magnetic ink character recognition (MICR) reader-sorter and magnetic tape units, is used to process cheque receipts and to store information from deposit slips. MICR is a scheme adopted by the banking industry for printing information on cheques that can be read by optical character recognition machines. Information on cheques such as the account number, bank code (branch number, etc.) and the amount of the cheque are read into the computer via the MICR reader-sorter. The computer then performs calculations and updates each active account in the master file of demand deposit accounts. The same application is envisaged for the developing nations. The software to perform such tasks is readily available.

Savings

The computerisation of savings accounts comes mainly in three forms:

(i) The first form does not dispense with the traditional passbook. Rather the information from the teller about a customer's account is entered into the computer via a CRT or other data entry mode and the customer's balance is automatically updated.

(ii) The second form does away with the traditional passbook and replaces it with a bank identification card. The account number on the card is printed in MICR characters. During each transactions (deposit or withdrawal) receipts are provided that indicate the amount involved in the current transaction and the total updated amount in the account.

(iii) In the third form, the tellers' or counter clerks' windows are equipped with data communications terminals which are linked to the bank's computer. This system automatically updates a customer's balance on the computer while it is updating the customer's passbook.

In most developing nations, the savings account is not very popular. One explanation may be that for a good majority of the population, there is really nothing to save. Another reason may be that people do not feel that their money is safe with the banks and hence it is not uncommon to find money stored away at home or in some perceived safe location.

Consumer loans

The main application of computers as regards consumer loan is in the area of consumer instalment credit loan accounting. The computer produces a daily transactions list, a weekly trial balance of all loan accounts, monthly statements, quarterly loan analysis, delinquency notices and other reports needed by loan officers and the consumer credit department.

Trust applications

In the management of corporate trusts, the computer is used to record changes in stock ownership, to calculate and print interest and dividend checks and reports, to provide year-end government dividends and interests reports. In the area of personal trust applications, the computer is used to handle accounts and to provide reports and documents required for additions and deletions to trust securities, portfolios, changes in market value of securities, trust and estate income, expenses etc.

Commercial loans

A data processing system for commercial loans automates the maintenance of records. The computer calculates new loan balance, the interest collected and earned, interest adjustments due to overpayment or underpayment. The system also produces a daily transactions list, individual note transactions report and customer liability summary report.

Automated teller machines (ATMs)

These are computer terminals or machines that, through the use of a plastic card and a personal identification number, give customers direct access to their accounts so that they are able to conduct regular banking transactions such as depositing funds in deposit or savings accounts, cashing cheques, making withdrawals, transferring funds between accounts and making account balance inquiries. Called 'any time tellers', because they are literally available for banking customers around the clock, they also bring the most commonly required banking services to customers where they are needed most – in shopping centres, on city streets, and even inside supermarkets. One ATM can handle over 25 000 transactions a month or about the workload of three human tellers. The central computer coordinates all transactions from every ATM that is on line to it and can keep track of every transaction at each individual terminal.

While some of the applications enumerated seem futuristic, it does not in any way minimise the impact that they can have on the economy or the productivity of a developing nation.

Applications in government

There is little doubt that systems thinking and automation through computerisation alone will not alleviate the maladies of the developing nations. However, when the capabilities of these instruments are examined in conjunction with the rapidly improving literacy rate in the developing nations, there is more than mere hope; there is optimism.

While government agencies in the developing nations lag behind most other establishments in responding to changes, it must be noted that there are legitimate reasons which dictate that government functionaries embrace innovation with some caution as compared to private organisations. In the operations of government agencies, there are some activities which defy characterisations and measurement with regard to efficiency and economy. This is true in the developing nations as well as the developed countries. However, as the role and specific functions of the government agencies have changed, the real question is whether current practices regarding information storage, retrieval and management are adequate. In the developing nations the amount of information that needs to be processed far outweigh the processing capability in almost all cases. Consequently information retrieval does present a real problem. A major reason for this is that all agencies are required to maintain files on most transactions. For instance the education ministry in most developing nations is responsible for administering scholarship awards for internal and overseas awardees. In most cases each award is for a duration of four years for undergraduate programs with a possibility of extension for graduate work. Over a ten year period and with awards made each year, the number of files maintained in such a situation even for a medium sized country is alarming to say the least. It should be noted that the scholarship administration function is only one of a host of other activities for which such an agency is responsible.

The application of computers in government, especially in information and data processing areas can have a significant impact on productivity in developing countries. As earlier indicated, a great deal of the activities of government agencies involve duplication in the areas of information collection, storage and retrieval efforts.

Some of the applications in government may include:

Information systems

A computerised information system is a useful tool for any arm of government whether in a developing country or a developed one. In developing countries, however, there is a lack of the data base needed to develop an effective and workable information system. In the area of vital statistics (birth and death) most of the data is maintained by individual families in family diaries. In such private files, they are worthless to the government. Such data of course is vital if a country is to adequately plan and budget for services, especially those that variously affect the different age groups. Vital statistics also enhance the ability of the government to estimate tax revenues, family incomes and more importantly population growth and changes.

A computerised information system is also useful for accounting purposes. A good accounting system provides a view of the government's financial situation. For a developing economy, it helps to show what programs are working and those that are not working. There is sometimes no doubt about the soundness or economic viability of some of the programs proposed or initiated by most developing nations. The problem, however, has been with the implementation and monitoring of the programs. A good accounting system will not stop cost overruns or help actual execution of the projects but it will at least show where the excesses and overruns exist.

Budgeting problems are a major concern in any economy but more so in a developing economy. A computerised budgeting system provides the flexibility of examining alternative budgets and budgetary constraints in the face of different wage and price increases and gross national product estimates.

Functional administrative areas

The contributions the computer can make to the development process can better be appreciated if examined in the light of the developed economies. Clearly the contributions that the computer has made to the productivity of the developed country is no longer a theory. In the developed nations, computers have been used somewhere and somehow in the administrative activities of all the federal, state and local governments. In this regard it is not an exaggeration to describe the governments of most developing nations as simply failing to adequately perform conventional and basic services. The answer to the problem may not lie in wholesale organisational changes. The answer may be to simply perform the usual daily business of government with proven modern methods. To do this requires a focus of expertise on data processing. The lack of expertise not only leaves the door open to misapplication, but it also breeds overselling and perpetuation of historical situations of monopoly. (Fite, 1965) The developing nation's experience has shown that such a situation has resulted in disillusionment not because the program is unsound but because the actual performance has not measured up to expectations.

The functional administration areas which could justify independent data processing installation will include:

Urban Planning   In urban planning a computer-based system can be used to provide central and city government planners with various alternatives of evaluating the effect of urban programs before such programs could be functional or implemented.

Criminal justice and public safety   A police computer system could be used to provide law enforcement officers with such information as outstanding warrants, criminal records and parole status.

Sanitation and waste management   This is perhaps an area in most developing nations that deserves a great deal of attention. In the developing countries, waste management is almost nonexistent. Waste collection is unorganised and irregular and waste disposal programs are even worse. In such situations, sanitation suffers and so does the health of the public. The development of integrated computer programs will be useful in developing and designing schedules for waste collection and sewage and water flows. The design of sewers and the estimate of the various cost components of a sanitary system could be greatly enhanced by the use of computers.

Traffic management Computers can be used to enhance traffic safety information such as accident records. Roadway traffic volumes obtained from automated data processing enables the administrators to make improvements on traffic flow and thus enhance traffic safety. Where needed computers can also be used in planning public transit systems specifically in such areas as forecasting traffic volumes and route changes.

Numerous benefits can be derived from the use of computers by the government and government functionaries. Some of these benefits include:

(i) *Cost savings*

Cost savings will be derived from the elimination of duplication, from increased productivity in information processing and from better utilisation of resources through planning. More comprehensive current and accurate information should result in better decisions.

(ii) *Increased revenues*

With a good information system, it is possible to have better audit, follow up, and uniform application of complex revenue and tax regulations. This will result in increased revenue. This is especially desirable in the developing nations where tax revenues are vital to national growth and development.

(iii) *Improved public service*

With a computerised system, various government services to the public should be improved and expanded. This is perhaps one of the most important benefits in a developing economy. The reason is that most public services are provided and supported by the government.

Applications in education

As the population of school-age children continues to grow in the developing nations, as the global literacy rate is lowered, and as more nations adopt the philosophy of viewing education as a continuous process, the commitment to education is bound to grow. Most educational leaders agree that current educational process is not efficient especially in the area of instruction and administration. The computer can play a vital role in improving efficiency in the educational process if properly used. This may be accomplished in the following ways:

Clerical and information handling

Computers are very applicable in this area for the same reason they are for industry. While education trails behind most of industry in computer usage, computers are being used in a variety of ways. Institutions use computers for classroom scheduling. Other applications include forecast and anticipation of future enrolments and in predicting staff and faculty requirements and resource levelling. While some of these applications are not yet found in the developing countries, it is hoped that the benefits will be no less significant than in the developed nations.

Computer aided instruction (CAI)

A major drawback of most educational systems is that whether in a developed or developing country teachers must deal with a class as a group rather than as individual students. Under this circumstance, it is simply impossible for the instructor to cater satisfactorily to the needs of both the slow and fast learners. One remedy for this situation is individualised instruction. However, due to the time involved, such an instruction scheme would be impossible without the use of computers. CAI will ensure that students will work at their own pace. It will not only help slower learners, it will encourage gifted students to proceed at their own pace and potential. This idea might seem futuristic for the developing nations. Even so it is important to recognise that it has a place in the educational development of these countries.

Research and development

In advanced economies the computer is a vital tool in conducting research and development in education as is the case in industry. Computers permit researchers to deal with complex problems in engineering, the physical sciences and even psychology. The same benefits can also be derived in the developing countries. One would not expect the full potential of the computers in research and development in a developing country to be realised as yet. However, it is important to note that improvements in current research and development effort can occur.

Health care systems

The application of computer and information processing technology to health care problems promises significant advances during the coming decades. One of the most distressing problems facing any developing nation is health care. While the average life span in the developed countries has been on the increase, the life span in the developing nations has remained constant or even decreased, and the infant mortality rate has remained high.

The computer will not solve these problems. However, it can help health planners provide timely and effective services. The developed nations' health record is an indication that the computer is a tremendous asset in facilitating health care delivery.

Typical applications of computers in health care systems for a developing nation will involve the automation of manual procedures for payroll, advance registration, menu planning and patient billing. Another important application, at least from the developed nations' experience, is in medical records keeping. A large amount of computerised medical data is of great value to medical research whether in a developing or developed nation. For most developing nations, another area that begs for computerisation is patient records. One visit to a public clinic in most developing nations may last a whole day. Most of this time is spent finding patient records. There is little doubt that the computer can have a significant impact on health care delivery in terms of improving the quality and level of services provided. The areas in which some of the gains or improvement might occur are in the following.

Scheduling

An automated (computerised) scheduling system may be utilised in the following manner:

 (i) Scheduling elective admissions
 (ii) Assigning patients to floors and beds
 (iii) Revising estimates of length of stay

(iv) Gathering data for revising and adjusting initial length of stay data

(v) Scheduling operating rooms and equipment

(vi) Scheduling equipment maintenance

Billing

The computer has become a vital tool in the development and implementation of financial information, patient accounting and statistics.

Menu planning

Menu planning and other dietary considerations have not received the attention they deserve in most developing nations. While this may not be the appropriate forum to address this problem, it is sufficient to point out that the health of a nation depends on what it ingests.

One of the goals of a good health care facility is to provide the proper diet for the patients. Consequently a well planned menu and dietary program is very essential to accomplish this goal. The computer can provide a great deal of assistance in planning a coherent menu system. Such a computer assisted program will help the dietician to:

(i)   Prepare recipes

(ii) Automatically update price information

(iii) Obtain menu nutrients and cost tallies by patient census and recipe, and by menu and day

(iv) Ensure that all available recipes are used in menu planning

(v)   Obtain food ingredient usage information

Purchasing

A computerised inventory and purchasing system is a vital tool in a health care system especially where the commodities are very diverse and numerous. Such a system is needed to:

(i)   Keep track of stock levels

(ii) Determine order quantities

(iii) Keep track of inventory costs

(iv) Update and track items in stock

Multiphasic health screening

This is a patient screening program whereby patients receive a periodic health examination in an automated multi-test laboratory. The equipment used for such a program will include an auto analyser, X-ray equipment, blood pressure, cardiograph and encephalograms. The information related to each test is stored on a computer. The computer then determines, using predetermined criteria, whether further tests or re-tests are necessary. The benefits of such a program for a developing nation is immeasurable.

Patient monitoring

In many developed nations it is now possible to carry out continuous patient monitoring. Such an on-line system has improved patient care especially with regard to such critical problems as the heart, lung and kidney. The system collects variable information, analyses it and displays both the measured and calculated values in real-time on a cathode ray tube (CRT). Typical variables measured are skin temperature, heart rate, brain activity, and blood pressure.

Blood banks

Blood is a critical commodity in any health care facility whether in Dakar, Senegal, West Africa or in Atlanta, Georgia, USA. Consequently a good accounting or recordkeeping system is vital especially with regard to initiating blood drives and the verification of the availability of blood types at a given hospital or at surrounding hospitals. The primary use of computers in this area is in blood inventory control. By linking computers in various hospitals together either by telephone lines or to a central computer, it is possible to poll each hospital daily to obtain the status and supply of blood. The data from such an inventory system enables blood to be dispatched quickly to places where it is needed.

Research

Some aspects of medical research today would be impossible without the use of computers. Computers are used in the collection and analysis of data. An important use of computers as a research tool is in the mathematical modelling and simulation that encompasses the investigators' theory of the function of a biological system. Such models enable the study of very complex systems and may also be a useful tool for instruction purposes. It is not too difficult to foresee similar use of the computer in the developing nations. The degree of application might vary but actual benefit will be the same.

Retailing

The problems of the retail industry in the developing economies are not unique to that industry but are identical to those of the other industries. The cost of carrying inventory, the cost of clerical help, and the cost of sales help have all risen. Many retail organisations in the developed nations have computer installations or have recognised the need for electronic data processing in a retail organisation. The same cannot be said of this industry in the developing nations. Most of the record keeping is manual and thus subject to all the problems typical of manual *vis-à-vis* automated operations. Information processing is thus very expensive in terms of man-hours and money.

The developed nations' experience has shown that the computer is not a tool just for heavy industry, manufacturing or big retail organisations. The prices of computers have been falling, and are at such levels that price is no longer a major limiting factor for those establishments who are serious about solving their information handling and storage problems.

For a developing country, some applications in the retail area will include:

Point-of-sale

This is the idea of mechanising data gathering so that data is entered into the system in a usable form whenever a sale or other type of transaction occurs. This idea has taken hold in the developed countries because of its advantages. The major benefits of this concept include the following:

1. Reduction of transcription errors
2. Faster data acquisition
3. Same data can be used for different applications without manual re-entry.

In general, point-of-sale systems provide a method of computing merchandise and sales audit information such as department, class, sales clerk identification, tax records on taxable items and the type of transaction.

Several types of equipment are now in use for point-of-sale data acquisition. There are currently two popular types in use: one that produces punched paper tape on the selling floor from information keyed into the cash register, and another that uses optical sensors to capture data from merchandise tags which contain optical or magnetic characters. In both cases, the information may be processed in-house or at a service bureau. Either type of equipment permits unlimited information entry and the keyboard can be designed to accommodate any desired information originating from the selling floor. Computer makers such as NCR, IBM (IBM 1285, 1232) and ITT all have good, low cost equipment for this purpose.

It is important to note that the benefits enumerated will accrue to a retail organisation whether in a developing nation or a developed one. The level of sophistication of the clients in the developing country might limit the extent of application but the same economies will be achieved.

8.6   ECONOMIC FEASIBILITY

The issue of the economic feasibility of acquiring a computer is vital and ought to be addressed. There is no doubt that the cost of equipment and hence the unit cost of processing data has been decreasing in an almost exponential fashion over the past few years. At this point in time, newer processing equipment is not only less expensive but also has more storage and operating capacities. Smaller standalone systems (microcomputers and minicomputers) are capable of providing computing power comparable with their bigger and more expensive counterparts (mainframes). In addition to hardware, there is a wide range of fully developed and tested applications software for almost all types of assignments. This software may be imported as it already exists, thus reducing conversion time and cost. It is also possible to develop software in-house to match the specific needs of the organisation.

While it is not suggested that procedures or computer software for specific applications be transplanted from the advanced countries to the developing ones, it is noteworthy that a computer software developed for a particular application in London, England may be used for the same application in Port Harcourt, Nigeria or Bombay, India.

Rather than an outright acquisition of an in-house computer, it may be advantageous to time-share a computer leased or bought by some other organisation. A vital task is to determine one's needs in terms of equipment and the level of automation warranted. It is also vital to review and analyse the system of the organisation so as to determine the current results and the information and results needed which are currently not available and the method to be used to produce these results. Another form of computer service other than outright acquisition is the service bureau. Service bureaus come in two main categories, namely the package bureau and the custom bureau. The package bureau has generalised software that in theory should be able to perform a lot of the basic needs such as payroll. The package bureaus are really not tailored to any particular client's needs but are general enough so that most clients are willing to adapt their specific needs to the services offered. The custom bureaus are much more flexible. They modify, enhance or adapt software to specific client needs and are of course more expensive. Such services are currently not available in most developing nations so outright acquisition might be the route to go.

8.7   SOCIAL IMPLICATIONS

In order to successfully make the necessary adjustment needed to accommodate the use of computers at any significant level, the most difficult changes must occur in the areas of human behaviour, attitudes and work ethic. The make up of human nature suggests that unless people can see a definite benefit that accrues when they change their working habits to something new and different, they will be unwilling to make the change. When this seemingly basic problem is combined with other forms of resistance such as fear of direct competition, then winning acceptance for the new way of doing things becomes a monumental task.

For a developing nation, training and maintaining qualified people to man a system once developed will be very difficult indeed.

8.8   CONCLUSIONS

While the computer and computerisation may provide assistance in manipulating data, the real problems rest with those individuals charged with the responsibility of making decisions based upon information obtained via the computer or from some other source. For example, the issues of morality, conflicting goals and values are not readily programmed and as such, decisions on such issues are for the most part subjective. It has been suggested that the tendency exists to belittle questions regarding these intangible but vital issues. While this may not be entirely true, it is apparent that the possibilities do exist for complex decisions involving human input and intervention to be made routine and thus there is the danger that they would then depend less on human reactions and judgements. This is of particular importance, especially in most developing nations where the issues of family, culture, and religion are treated in an almost sacred fashion. This danger, however, should not overshadow the equally vital issue, which is the possibility that computers and electronics technology will aid decision-makers, especially those of the developing nation, in making and executing wise and more informed decisions.

References

ALFORD, B. G., COLVIN, F. E. (eds) (1970) *Hospital Electronic Data Processing Journal Articles* (Medical Examination Publishing Co., Inc.).

BERNSTEIN, J. B. (ed.) (1976) *Computers in Public Administration* (Oxford: Pergamon Press).

COLTON, K. W., KRAEMER, L. K. (eds) (1968) *Computers and Banking* (Boston Bankers Publishing Co.).

DAMACHI, U. G. (1970) *Nigerian Modernization, The Colonial Legacy* (New York: The Third Press).

DANZIGER, J. N., DUTTAN, W. H., KLING, R., KRAEMER, K. L., (1982) *Computers and Politics* (Columbia University Press, 1982).

FITE, H. H. (1965) *The Computer Challenge to Urban Planners and Administrators* (New York: Spartan Books, MacMillan, 1965).

HEARLE, E., MASON, R. J. (1963) *A Data Processing System for State and Local Governments* (Englewood Cliffs, New Jersey: Prentice-Hall, Inc.).

HOOS, IDA (1960) 'The Impact of Office Automation on Workers', *International Labour Review*, Vol. 82, No. 4, October.

LUCAS, H. C. (1981) *The Analysis, Design and Implementation of Information Systems* (New York: McGraw-Hill Book Company).

LYNCH, R., RICE, J. (1977) *Computers: Their Impact and Use* (New York: Holt, Rinehart and Winston).

Manpower Research Unit (1966) Fourth Report, 'Computers in Offices', included in Organization for Economic Cooperation and Development (OECD), Manpower Aspect of Automation and Technical Change, Zurich.

Papers presented at the Retail Research Institute, 7th Annual EDP Conference For Retailers, San Francisco, 1965.

ROSA, N., ROSA, S. (1980) *Small Computers for the Small Businessman* (Blue Ridge Summit, PA: TAB Books, Inc.).

SAGASTI, F. R. (1974) 'Operations Research in the Context of Underdevelopment: Some Case Studies from Peru', *Operational Research Quarterly*, Vol. 25, No. 7.

SARDINAS, J. (1981) *Computing Today: An Introduction to Business Data Processing* (Englewood Cliffs, NJ: Prentice-Hall, Inc.).

SHELL, R. L., DAMACHI, N. A. (1980) 'Managing the Industrial Engineering Function in Developing Countries: The Role of the IE', Institute of Industrial Engineers Annual Conference Proceedings, May.

SHELL, R. L., SHUPE, D. S. (1978) 'Productivity: Hope for City Woes', *Productivity: A Series from Industrial Engineering*, M. E. Mundel (ed.) (American Institute of Industrial Engineers).

TAVISS, I. (1970) *The Computer Impact* (Englewood Cliffs, NJ: Prentice-Hall, Inc.).

USBLS United States Bureau of Labor Statistics (1980).

USBLS United States Bureau of Labor Statistics (1981).

WALKER, K. A. (1967) 'Automation and Nonmanual Workers', Labour and Automation Bulletin, No. 5 (Geneva: International Labor Office, 1967).

9 Computer Applications in Information Retrieval and Writing for Technology Transfer

William Leigh and Michael Berry

9.1 COMPUTER-AIDED RESEARCH AND WRITING

The computer, and especially the personal computer, has potential as an aid to the type of knowledge work known as research and writing. This chapter describes this capability as it exists now and suggests where this capability may be extended in the future. The scope embraced includes the processes of composing (information collecting, organising, and synthesising) and producing (text keyboarding, editing, and formatting) research reports, especially those reports which involve bibliographic searches as in technology transfer. Figure 9.1 is a block diagram of the flow of the processes of composing and producing research articles and reports. The computer can be a tool to accelerate and augment these processes, or it can be a full-fledged assistant.[1]

Developing nations have acute needs to transfer technology. An effective tool for this task, which has become possible with computers, is the accessing of technical bibliographic databases. This chapter describes how computers may be used to enhance that process of technology transfer which is accomplished by information retrieval and technical report writing.

9.2 INFORMATION RETRIEVAL

Since the 1960s, when the enabling computer technology became available, many bibliographic citation and full-text databases covering almost any area of knowledge have been built and made available for access with computer terminal equipment via telephone lines. Figure 9.2 is a diagram of this arrangement. Lancaster[2] supplies a

Figure 9.1 Flow of information and tasks in the composition and production of a technical research report

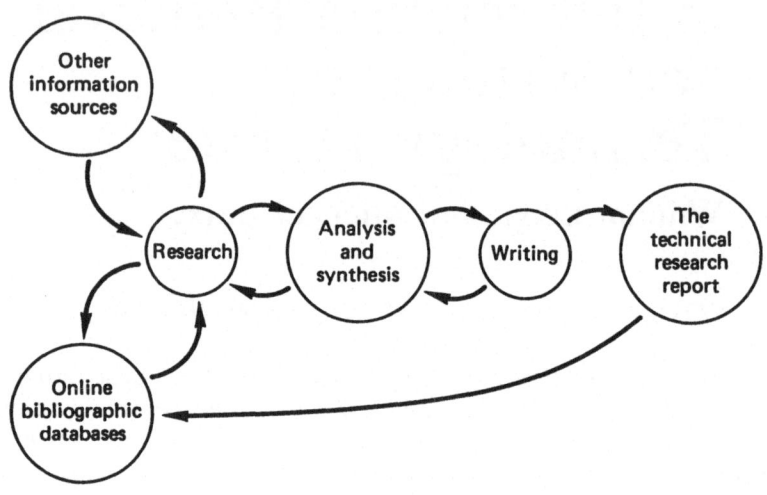

Figure 9.2 Online information retrieval

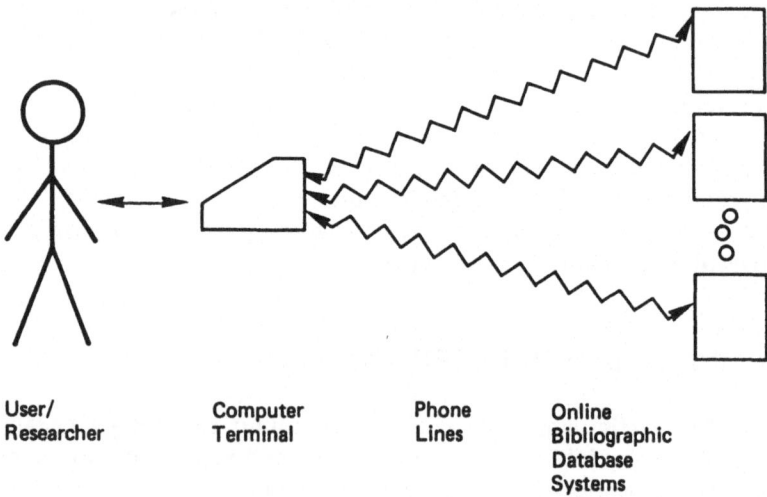

Table 9.1   Some major databases and their subjects

ABI/INFORM	Business and Economics
AGRICOLA	Agriculture and Related Subjects
COMPENDEX	Worldwide Coverage of Engineering
ERIC	Educational Materials
INSPEC	Physics, Electrotechnology, Computers
MEDLINE	Medicine, Dentistry, Nursing

good overview of the history and capabilities of information retrieval systems. Salton[3] offers a survey of technical developments in the field.

Bibliographic databases contain citation entries composed of titles, authors, publication information, and abstracts of articles, books, and reports. Full-text databases contain the complete texts of the documents in addition. There is one entry in these databases for each document. Usually the databases specialise in one area of knowledge. Glossbrenner[4] is a directory to the most widely available databases, what they contain, and how they are accessed. Table 9.1 contains a list of some major databases and a description of their contents. Wente[5] describes one bibliographic database system in detail.

Entries are accessed with keywords. Keywords are supplied for the documents by the author, by a human indexer, or with automatic methods. Figure 9.3 contains a citation including keywords which might be from a computer science bibliographic database.

Queries are formulated by the researcher to access databases. These queries must be expressed in the special language supported by the specific database. Efforts are underway to standardise these languages across databases. The International Organization for Standardization (ISO) is considering one such standard language as described in the 'Draft Specification for Commands for Interactive Search Systems'.[6] Figure 9.4 contains several queries expressed in this draft standard query language. Another solution to the problem of multiple querying languages which does not involve changing the database systems themselves is the 'gateway' approach. Marcus[7] has built such a system which uses a computer to convert queries specified in a standard language to the specific languages of the individual database systems. Figure 9.5 shows the relationship of the components in the 'gateway' approach to online information retrieval.

Figure 9.3   Citation from a typical bibliographic database

Title	– A Data Structure for Word Processing
Author	– Jones, John M.
Date	– August, 1982
Source	– Journal of Computer Science
Pages	– 354–368
Keywords	– DATA STRUCTURES, WORD PROCESSING, OFFICE AUTOMATION, TEXT PROCESSING, TEXT EDITING
Abstract	– A data structure is presented which has desirable properties in situations requiring automatic justification under conditions of insert and over-write. This situation occurs in screen-oriented word-processing systems. Examples of use and test results are reported.

Figure 9.4   Example queries

FIND WORD PROCESSING AND DATA STRUCTURES
FIND (WORD PROCESSING OR TEXT PROCESSING) AND TEXT EDITING
FIND (DATA STRUCTURES OR ALGORITHMS) AND WORD PROCESSING
FIND TEXT EDITING AND DATE 1977

The major skill required in formulating queries is picking the keywords to specify for the search. Not only must the keywords chosen match the requirements and interests of the searcher, but they must also be consistent with the indexing vocabulary of the database. An option which is becoming more popular as computer processing power becomes cheaper is the full-text search for keywords . Rather than confining the search to the keywords formally assigned to the documents, the searcher instructs the system to search the abstracts, or even the documents' full texts, for the presence of particular words, word origins, or for the presence of multiple words which occur in a specified proximity.

Modern information retrieval systems offer facilities for rapid and exhaustive generation of bibliographies and location of source materials for research. This is a use of computers for accelerating knowledge work. Developments in this area are beginning to make this capability available to knowledge workers who cannot invest in the training and experience now required to access multiple databases effectively. Such improvements in the man-machine interface

Figure 9.5   Diagram of a 'gateway' architecture

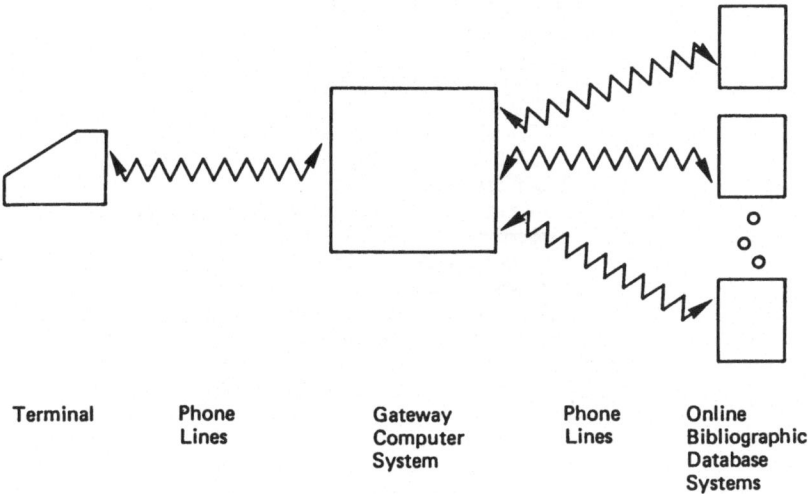

| Terminal | Phone
Lines | Gateway
Computer
System | Phone
Lines | Online
Bibliographic
Database
Systems |

to information retrieval systems are taking the form of standard, more 'user-friendly' languages and 'gateway' computer system architectures.

9.3   REVIEW AND ANALYSIS OF CITATIONS

Citations once retrieved from a database may be delivered to the searcher on paper or 'down-loaded' in computer-readable form to his 'gateway' or personal computer. The task now is to determine which citations are relevant and which citations are promising enough to justify ordering the document, and then to classify the relevant citations into sub-areas of the research topic. The computer can accelerate this task. Some aspects of this task may even be delegated to the computer.

Figure 9.6 shows an example of a terminal display screen which might be presented by a typical citation review program. At the bottom of the screen is a 'menu' of possible operations to be selected by the reviewer. According to that menu, pressing the RETURN key presents the next citation in the file. Selecting '0' option allows the operator to assign categories to the citation. These categories might

Figure 9.6   Example of REVIEW terminal display

Title	– A Data Structure for Word Processing
Author	– Jones, John M.
Date	– August, 1982
Source	– Journal of Computer Science
Pages	– 354–368
Keywords	– DATA STRUCTURES, WORD PROCESSING, OFFICE AUTOMATION, TEXT PROCESSING, TEXT EDITING
Abstract	– A data structure is presented which has desirable properties in situations requiring automatic justification under conditions of insert and over-write. This situation occurs in screen-oriented word-processing systems. Examples of use and test results are reported.

USER-ASSIGNED CATEGORIES: INTRODUCTORY, ORDER

MENU:	RETURN	– next citation
	0	– assign categories
	1	– search on literal

be topic-specific assigned at the discretion of the reviewer or they might be of other significance, such as 'ORDER' for a document to be ordered in its full-text version. The '1' option allows the reviewer to search the citation file for the presence of words or phrases.

The possibility of an automatic method of determining the relevance of documents or abstracts has been an object of research in information science for some time.[8] One approach to this uses the lexical association methods which have their origin in the work of Luhn.[9] Luhn observed that the significant terms in a document were neither the most frequent nor the least frequent terms in the document. Other researchers have developed this observation and its derivatives into methods for automatic abstracting and automatic keyword generation.[10]

As the abstracts which are the result of a search are already homogeneous in content, the most frequently appearing words in the collection (after discarding a 'stop list' of common words which have little meaning such as 'a', 'an', 'the', and so forth) should indicate the overall nature and purpose of the search. So abstracts which contain these words can be considered consistent with the purpose of the search, and therefore relevant. A ranking of the members of the set of citations resulting from a search may be accomplished by considering as more relevant the citations whose abstracts contain more of these frequent words. This method can be more effective if the frequent words to be used in the ranking are first displayed on the terminal display for the operator to review and discard if, by chance, they are not relevant as intended.

After the citations are ranked, they can be reviewed in order with the REVIEW facility described above. It is desirable that they be reviewed in order of decreasing relevance score. This allows the researcher, when he is satisfied that enough citations have been reviewed, to terminate the reviewing session with some assurance that the remaining citations are of lesser relevance than the ones reviewed directly.

Automatic relevance ranking is an example of the delegation of some of the substance of the research process to the computer. Such a computer-aided process as this can be effective in reducing the work required to manually review many abstracts. This type of pre-ranking is only feasible with the aid of a computer.

9.4 ORGANISATION OF INFORMATION AND IDEAS

It is in the organisation and synthesis of information to promote the generation of ideas that the computer may eventually make its main contributions. Bush[11] anticipated this use of a computer technology in 1945, although such technology did not exist then. Bush's MEMEX system, as it was proposed, allowed the structuring of documents into an arbitrarily deep outline structure and the reuse of document segments by linking them into new documents with 'trails', or connections between similar subjects in different documents.

The MEMEX ideas have been re-proposed repeatedly and have achieved many implementations. A recent implementation is Price's THUMB system.[12] In the THUMB system, experts prepare multithreaded indexes for documents so that readers can peruse the document at different levels of detail and investigate different aspects directly.

The THUMB system is an example of how a computer-based system can augment the powers of a researcher in the substance of his work. Expertly prepared THUMB indexes can present a document to a new reader in a manner which directly meets his needs.

'Knowledge graphs', which is a modern term for the types of structures used by THUMB, can become the basis for a 'knowledge support environment'.[13] In the context of the analysis and organisation of bibliographic citations, the automatic creation of a knowledge graph for a retrieved citation set would facilitate the understanding of a field of knowledge and the interactions between and among the documents. It is not likely that this can be accomplished effectively with lexical association or syntactical methods. The realisation of this ambition will wait for the development of adequate natural language semantic understanding methods in artificial intelligence. However, these structures might be developed manually for textbooks or for seminal technical articles, or a researcher could build such a structure to support his own personal endeavours.

One application for knowledge graphs which has not been investigated is as a vehicle for the presentation of the keyword vocabulary of a bibliographic database. This could aid researchers in finding proper terms for searching and in becoming acquainted with the area of coverage of the database. Also, as the researcher followed the graph, he could designate keywords encountered as important to him or not. The system could formulate a search query from this trail.

The augmentation of human ability to organise information and generate ideas is a great potential of the personal computer. This capability will need to be achieved by the availability of many different tools which can be selected for use and extended to the needs of individual researchers. This capability will only be achieved by a symbiosis between the personal computer and the research/ writer.

9.5 ARTIFICIAL INTELLIGENCE FOR RESEARCH AND WRITING

Machine translation between natural languages is an older ambition of artificial intelligence. Systems now exist which augment and accelerate a human translator's effectiveness. This is an example of the symbiotic type of man-machine cooperative system. The capability of semi- or fully automatic machine translation has obvious benefits for researchers and writers.

A special case of machine translation is the automatic answering of natural language questions directed against a database. A system which functions in this manner is a special type of 'gateway', one which mediates between a natural language, such as English, and the formal query language of the database system. Figure 9.7 is a dia-

Figure 9.7   An organisation for a system with a natural language question-answering component

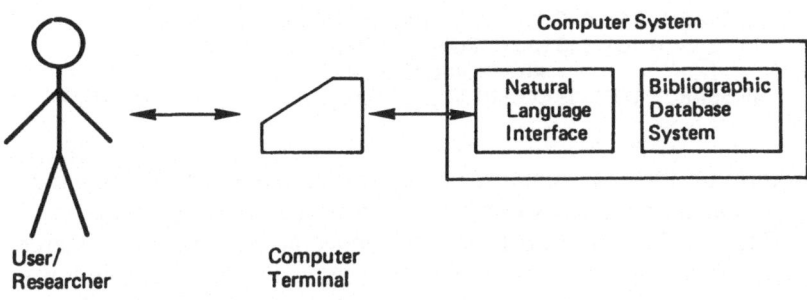

gram of a possible relationship between the functional part of such a system.

A desirable attribute of natural language database question-answering systems is 'cooperativeness'.[14] This term denotes the behaviour which answers the query 'How many articles are about alternative energy sources?' not with '5' but with 'There are only 5, but this database contains information only on agriculture'. This type of behaviour requires abilities beyond language translation. Also needed are self-knowledge, and the facility to call it up when appropriate.

Such a natural language question-answering system would be beneficial to researchers beyond conventional information retrieval. However, it will probably be some time before it is realised. With such systems of lesser skill, there would be considerable danger in attributing the system with greater knowledge and skill than it actually possesses. Artificial intelligence systems may seduce humans into suspending their own critical reasoning capacity. This is a greater problem because one of the greatest unsolved problems in artificial intelligence is to construct systems that know the limits of their own knowledge, that is, that know when they do not know.

An artificial intelligence technique which can be adapted to endow a system with self-knowledge is the 'expert system'. The expert system is close to wide-spread commercial application.[15] An expert system has been built[16] to guide researchers in the selection of bibliographic databases for searching. Figure 9.8 shows some possible examples of 'rules' which might be used in such a system. The computer-based expert system carries on a dialogue with the user to

Figure 9.8   Some rules for a computer-based expert system to guide database selection

> IF SEARCH TOPIC IS AGRICULTURE THEN USE AGRICOLA
> IF SEARCH TOPIC IS ELECTRONICS AND AGRICULTURE THEN USE
> AGRICOLA AND INSPEC
> IF SEARCH TOPIC IS COMPUTERS THEN USE INSPEC OR COMPENDEX

determine the requirements of the search. These requirements are vetted against the rules to result in recommended databases.

The possibilities of artificial intelligence are exciting for researchers and writers. The future of such systems is not to replace but to augment human skills. Presently, such systems exist mainly in laboratories and in most cases can augment only the skills of the non-expert. Indeed, artificial intelligence systems may never truly augment the skills of real experts but only accelerate the accomplishment of some tasks. The great advantage of these systems may be in giving non-experts some semi-expert abilities through a working mode of symbiosis and mutual consultation.

9.6   INTERACTIVE EDITING SYSTEMS

Screen-oriented text-editors are now commonly available with personal computers, and this type of system is nearly universally preferred. Such a system allows the user to key and manipulate text on a computer screen and to see what the finished version will look like at all times.

Before the advent of the personal computer and its fast response and screen display, the standard for computer text editing was the command-oriented editor. Such systems were adapted to the constraints imposed by a connection to the computer over telephone lines which supported only slow data rates and by the then-standard terminal, the line-at-a-time typewriter terminal. Command-oriented, line-based editors refer to text by a computer-assigned line number. That line number must be referenced when modifying the text.

Screen-oriented editors allow the text to be modified directly on the screen. The particular text to be modified is pointed out with a cursor character on the screen which is moved about with special cursor control keys or with a special auxiliary input device for this

Table 9.2   Unix 'Writer's Workbench' commands

ABST	Score text abstractness
ACRO	Find acronyms (words developed from the initial letters of names)
FINDBE	Identify awkward grammar
PARTS	Assign parts of speech
SEXIST	Locate sex-biased phrases
SPELLWB	Check spelling

purpose. (One such special device for pointing is the 'mouse', which is moved about the table surface to move the cursor about the screen.) These screen-oriented editors are generally accepted to be faster and more effective than the line-oriented editors, but they do require more elaborate equipment.

Somewhere between an information and idea organisation tool and an interactive editing tool is the 'structure' type of editor.[17] A text editor works with normal text in terms of words, characters, and lines. A structure editor works with documents, sections, paragraphs, and so forth. The writer must specify a structure for his document, or take one which is already prepared on the system. The structure editor can help a writer work in a top-down manner from an outline. Sub-parts can be promoted, demoted, or rearranged in the structure.

After the text is structured and exists in the computer in a semi-finished form, there are still tasks the computer can perform for the writer. The computer can aid the writer by checking his spelling, checking his punctuation, and even checking his grammar. The Unix 'Writer's Workbench'[18] is a computer system which contains facilities for many of these writing aids. Table 9.2 is a list of some of the 'Writer's Workbench' commands with summaries of what they do.

An example of a text-manipulating computer system which fully exploits advanced screen-oriented techniques is the Xerox '8010 Star Information System'.[19] This system organises its screen like the top of an office desk. On this screen 'desktop', the computer can display both sides of a regular-sized piece of typing paper simultaneously with a number of 'icons'. The icons each signify one of various operations that can be performed such as 'delete a document', or 'catalogue a document'. The icon for 'catalogue a document', for example, might be a picture of an office filing cabinet. The most meaningful icon may be the wastepaper receptacle which signifies deleting a document. The mouse is used to select spots on the pages for typing new or modified text as well as to pick icons to cause the computer to carry out operations.

Icons are a pictographic method for implementing 'menus'. A menu is a list of options presented to the user on the screen for selection. This is different from a command-driven interface in that the user's choices for the next operation are available for selection on the screen. In 'menus' only the operations shown are allowed. It requires skill to design a menu-driven system to be certain that the operations required by the user at any point are available on the current menu.[20]

The use of the screen to show how the finished document will look aids writers, especially where the arrangement and graphics are complex. The 'desk-top' and 'menu-driven' models for computer interaction are simple and easily learned by people who do not wish to become adept at conventional computer command methods. This development will facilitate training for computer use in developing countries. For a complete survey of these interactive editing approaches see Meyrowitz and van Dam, *Interactive Editing Systems*[21, 22]. These more effective user modes require what was once expensive computer equipment, but this capability is now made economically possible by the mass availability of personal computers.

9.7 A COMPUTER-BASED PERSONAL RESEARCH AND WRITING ENVIRONMENT

Combining the above-described facilities on a modern, large-capacity personal computer results in a computer-based environment which is supportive of the work of an individual researcher/writer. This personal computer can be a 'gateway' to bibliographic and full-text databases, allowing its user to draw material and references over communications lines from any database in the world. Tools can be brought to bear to analyse and organise this raw material of research. New material can be integrated into the researcher's own 'knowledge graph' for his domain of interest or entered into his own bibliographic database.[23] A structure editor can be used to synthesise research materials and ideas into new documents.

These functions can be accessed with a 'desk-top' model screen display which allows more than one activity to be pursued at once. Bibliographic citations could be reviewed and classified and placed in an outline document structure at the same time. The weaving of these new materials into the researcher's 'knowledge graph' could be interleaved with the other work. A capability for interleaving sub-tasks allows the researcher to proceed with his work in an order natural to the task and to the researcher. Features such as on-screen high-lighting and annotation which are special requirements of research and writing work could be included.

This system should be 'open', that is, allowing the addition and subtraction of tools from the toolset according to the wishes of the individual user. The initial set of tools supplied with a copy of the system should be selected or developed to apply directly to the information retrieval and writing problem.

9.8 THE CIRCLE CLOSES

The researcher's new document can be added to the bank of knowledge through 'electronic publishing'. As documents were downloaded, they can be up-loaded to bibliographic and full-text databases or transferred directly to other researchers, thus closing the research and writing circle.

The tools and methods outlined in this chapter exist in prototype or commercial versions on various personal computers, but are usually used in isolation. Efforts of the highest quality continue to integrate these tools into systems which not only accelerate but augment humans in doing knowledge work.

Research and writing are certainly a profitable area for the application of computers. It is to be anticipated that in the 1990s, perhaps the greatest progress in the application of computers will occur in these areas.

References

1. Lefrere, P. 'Text Processing,' in T. O'Shea and M. Eisenstadt (eds) *Artificial Intelligence*, (New York: Harper and Row 1984).
2. Lancaster, F. *Information Retrieval Systems*, (New York: Wiley-Interscience 1979).
3. Salton, G. 'Automatic Information Retrieval', *Computer*, September, 1980, p. 41–56.
4. Glossbrenner, A. *Personal Computer Communications* (New York: St. Martin's Press 1983).
5. Wente, V. 'NASA/RECON and user interface considerations', in

D. Walker (ed.) *Interactive Bibliographic Search: The User/Computer Interface*, (Montvale, New Jersey: AFIPS Press, 1971) pp. 95–104.

6. International Organization for Standardization (ISO), 'Draft Specification for Commands for Interactive Search Systems', May, 1984, Document ISO/TC 46/4/5 N46.

7. Marcus, R. 'User Assistance in Bibliographic Retrieval Networks Through a Computer Intermediary', *IEEE Transactions on System, Man, and Cybernetics*, Vol. SMC-12, No. 2, March/April 1982, pp. 116–32.

8. Maron, M., and Kuhns, J. 'On Relevance: Probabilistic Indexing and Information Retrieval', *Journal of Association for Computing Machinery*, Vol. 7, 1960, pp. 216–44.

9. Luhn, H. 'A Statistical Approach to Mechanized Encoding and Searching of Literary Information', *IBM Journal*, October, 1957, pp. 309–17.

10. Salton, G. *A Theory of Indexing*, Society for Industrial and Applied Mathematics, 1975.

11. Bush, V. 'As We May Think,' *Atlantic Monthly* 176(7), pp. 101–108.

12. Price, L. 'Thumb: An Interactive Tool for Accessing and Maintaining Text', IEEE *Transactions on Systems, Man, and Cybernetics* Vol. SMC-12, No. 2, March/April 1982, pp. 155–161.

13. Wegner, P. 'Capital-Intensive Software Technology', *Computer*, July, 1984, pp. 4–45.

14. Kaplan, S. 'On the Difference Between Natural Language and High Level Query Languages', Proceedings of the ACM 78, Washington, D.C.

15. Nau, D. 'Expert Systems', *Computer*, February, 1983, pp. 63–85.

16. Yip, Man-Kam 'An Expert System for Document Retrieval', M.S. Thesis in Electrical Engineering and Computer Science, MIT, Cambridge, MA., February, 1981.

17. Walker, J. 'The Document Editor: A Support Environment for Preparing Technical Documents', Proceedings of the ACM SIGOA Symposium on Text Manipulation, June 8–10, 1981, in SIGOA *Newsletter*, Vol. 2, No. 1 and 2, Spring/Summer, 1981, pp. 44–50.

18. MacDonald, N., Frase, L., and Keenan, S. 'Writer's Workbench: Computer Programs for Text Editing and Assessment', (Piscateway, New Jersey: Bell Laboratories, 1980).

19. Smith, D., Irby, C., Kimball, R., Verplank, B., and Harslem, E. 'Designing the Star User Interface', *Byte*, Vol. 7, No. 4, April, 1982, pp. 242–282.

20. Robertson, G., MacCracken, D., and Newell, A. 'The ZOG Approach to Man-Machine Communication', *International Journal of Man-Machine Studies* Vol. 14, 1981, p. 461–488.

21. Meyrowitz, N., and Van Dam, A. 'Interactive Editing Systems: Part I', *Computing Surveys*, Vol. 14, No. 3, September, 1982, pp. 321–352.

22. Meyrowitz, N., and Van Dam, A. 'Interactive Editing Systems: Part II', *Computing Surveys*, Vol. 14, No. 3, September, 1982, pp. 353–415.

23. Bertram, D., and Bader, C. 'Storage and Retrieval of Bibliographic References Using a Microprocessor System', *International Journal of Bio-medical Computing*, Vol. 11, 1980, pp. 285–293.

10 Database Management and Application Systems for Managers and Accountants

William Leigh and Michael Doherty

10.1 INTRODUCTION

Today's proliferation of cheap computing power has sparked a demand for applications software that cannot be met by traditional program development techniques. One answer to this problem is to allow and even require the end-users, the managers and accountants who ultimately use the computer, to implement their own systems. It is expected that this is possible and even inevitable (whether systems professionals want it or not) as appropriate tools are developed and become available.[1, 2, 3] Forward-looking managers in developing countries should take advantage of these developments – both personally and in their organisations.

In the past, most update and retrieval processing against a database has been done via a high-level programming language such as COBOL. It is more common now for retrieval to be accomplished using a self-contained, query-processing language directly, especially in relational model database management systems. In the future, as such systems become more widely available, it is probable that the data processing functions of editing and posting associated with updating master files also will be accomplished with high-level interfaces rather than through a host language such as COBOL. This paper considers implementing data processing completely in the style of high-level database query and manipulation facilities.

Such end-user development tools are an ongoing area of development. The oldest type of tool is the report generator such as RPG and MARK IV. A newer version of the report generation idea is the 'by-example' approach.[4] However, capability to do more than query and report from existing databases must exist. This may involve the

159

designing of a domain-specific language[5] or the integration of a database management system with a procedural language.[6]

Of course, end-user tools must be easy to use. This means the purpose of the tools must closely follow the functionality understood and employed by the end-user, who in our case is the manager or accountant. Additional objectives are to develop end-user programming facilities which:

(a)   support non-procedural (descriptive systems design);
(b)   work with high-level, aggregate data objects where possible (instead of low-level characters, fields, and records);
(c)   are organised as a library of high-level, reusable components (so that once a function is working, it need not be re-developed).

One approach to developing these tools is to adapt the facilities of a relational database management system (DBMS) to the requirements of end-user programming for business. The relational DBMS is chosen as a base because it is well-defined,[7] is close conceptually to a manager or accountant's 'natural' concept of data,[8] and because it lends itself to a high-level non-procedural approach to data processing. Also, relational database design is understood well enough to be taught at a rudimentary level to end-users.[9]

The chapter proceeds by developing the ideas in a bottom-up fashion. First, a description of DBMS's and their facilities is supplied for background. Particular aspects of the relational-style of DBMS are described in some detail. Then possible mechanisms for the basic data processing function of handling transactions are presented. This is followed by an example of the executable application schema approach, making use of the machinery previously described.

10.2   BACKGROUND – DATABASE MANAGEMENT SYSTEMS

Managerial and accounting data processing requires much file processing. The database management system (DBMS) is a type of computer program which aids file-processing by storing information about the files involved in several applications (a database) in one common file. This common file, called a 'data dictionary', can be accessed for information about the structure of the information stored in the database. This data dictionary can be used by the application programs to separate their logical processing from the physical form of the data files. When an application program requires a piece of information from the database, it can query the DBMS for the physical form and storage location of that information. The DBMS finds this information in the data dictionary.

Thus, when the physical structure of the database is changed by adding fields to a file, by lengthening a field, and so forth, the application programs do not need to be changed. This change in the structure of the database is recorded in the data dictionary. Then, whenever the changed fields of the database are accessed, the new form of them will be used by the DBMS and, hence, the application programs. This avoids maintenance of application programs for many types of file changes.

Database management systems are characterised by the 'data model' which they support. The 'data model' is a system for structuring and accessing data. Some such models for data are amenable to what professional programmers do, and others are more agreeable to the ways of looking at data used by end-users.

A data dictionary typically lists the file-like pieces of the databases and the field-like pieces within them and serves as a codifying place for the database and the names used to name its parts. When the data dictionary is also used to contain data-model-specific information, it may be called a database 'schema'.

Data-model-specific information can be specifications to be used by the DBMS for maintaining the 'integrity' of the data in the database. One type of integrity is 'key-integrity' which means that the DBMS is to police, for example, the records in a bank account file to be sure that two people do not have the same account number assigned to them. Another type of integrity is 'referential integrity', which refers to the DBMS checking for such things as the use of an incorrect code in a record. A list of valid codes is kept to be automatically referred to by the DBMS in maintaining this type of integrity.

Database management systems are a technical tool used by computer information systems professionals. However, the application-oriented extensions to database management systems presented in this chapter make them a direct ally of the manager and accountant as well.

10.3   THE RELATIONAL DATA MODEL AND RELATIONAL ALGEBRA

Relational database management systems are so named because they employ the relational model of data. In the relational model data are organized into 'relations', or tables. A relation is a set of 'tuples', or rows. The columns have names, or 'attributes'. In a relation some subset of the attributes functions as a key, that is, contains a value which is a unique identifier of the row within the table. The attribute values in a relation consist of all the elements in the column of the relation corresponding to that attribute name. Typically a relation is defined:

relation name (attribute, . . ., attribute).

The set of operators used for manipulating the data in a database is called a data manipulation language. Because querying is a predominant function, they are also called query languages. Three main families of languages can be identified: relational algebra languages, predicate calculus-oriented languages, and mapping-oriented languages. This discussion is based on a relational algebra approach to the query language.

Many relational algebra operators and differing versions of them have been defined and variously implemented.[10] The ones of interest here include SELECT, PROJECT, SORT, SUMMARY, DIFFERENCE, and JOIN. SELECT operates on a single relation to retrieve a subset of the rows. PROJECT operates on a single relation to retrieve columns. SORT, of course, sequences a relation based on the values in particular columns. SUMMARY acts on a single relation to reduce its number of rows to those with specified unique attribute values and to total certain other attribute values. DIFFERENCE compares two relations and outputs a third relation which contains tuples of the first relation which do not have matching key values in the second relation. JOIN combines two relations in a specific way to produce a third.

For example, consider the relation and the attribute values:

Relation A0 (name, bank-balance, account-type)

PHIL	212	DEPOSIT
JACK	118	DEPOSIT
SUE	311	SAVINGS

The operation SELECT FROM A ACCOUNT-TYPE = "DEPO-SIT" GIVING A1 results in:

Relation A1 (name, bank-balance, account-type)

| PHIL | 212 | DEPOSIT |
| JACK | 118 | DEPOSIT |

The operation PROJECT FROM A NAME, BANK-BALANCE GIVING A2 results in:

Relation A2 (name, bank-balance)

PHIL	212
JACK	118
SUE	311

If we have another relation:

Relation B (account-type, average-bank-balance)

| DEPOSIT | 215 |
| SAVINGS | 112 |

the operation JOIN A TO B ON ACCOUNT-TYPE GIVING AB results in:

Relation AB (name, bank-balance, account-type, average bank-balance)

PHIL	212	DEPOSIT	215
JACK	118	DEPOSIT	215
SUE	311	SAVINGS	112

The operation SUMMARY A BY ACCOUNT-TYPE FOR BANK-BALANCE GIVING A3 results in:

Relation A3 (name, bank-balance, account-type)

| - - - - | 330 | DEPOSIT |
| - - - - | 311 | SAVINGS |

(The values of attributes which are neither totalled nor used for control in a SUMMARY are usually undefined.) The operation DIFFERENCE A to A1 GIVING A4 results in:

Relation A4 (name, bank-balance, account-type)

SUE   311   SAVINGS

A utility to create and maintain relations is usually provided with a relational DBMS. We call this operator MAINTAIN. It takes as its argument a relation name. The relation name and its attributes must be previously defined in the data dictionary.

The relational database management system is a type of database management which is conceptually accessible to non-systems professionals such as managers and accountants. The relational database management system will be a base for the application of specific tools presented in the rest of this paper.

10.4   EXPRESSING DATA PROCESSING FUNCTIONS WITH RELATIONAL OPERATORS

Management and accounting data processing applications involve the functions of creating, listing (or reporting), and updating files. Variations of listing include detail, exception, summary, and control break reporting. It is apparent that most desired reports (except those requiring computation other than totalling) can be generated using the relational operators listed above.

A relation of transactions could be created with MAINTAIN. The requirement of data processing applications for the posting of those transactions is not directly addressed by the relational algebra, however. Combinations of operators do not seem to bring about the desired result either. The desired post-type operation does not seem to be available as a primitive or as a combination of primitives in any of the benchmark relational database management systems described in major textbooks.[11, 12]

The following sub-sections contain explanations of alternative methods for achieving adequate data processing functionality within the framework of a relational database management system.

Batch processing extensions

To the relational algebra operators described, add the operators EDIT and POST. EDIT is to be a synonym for a type of DIFFER-ENCE with the first relation argument to be the transaction file and the second to be the master file. An additional argument to the EDIT is a list of attributes to be used as a key when referencing the master relation. The key of the master relation is assumed to be in a like number of leftmost attributes. POST (named after the similar ac-counting operation) is to be an operator which causes the transac-tions in the relation used as the first argument to be 'posted' to the master file, which is the relation used as the second argument. Other arguments of POST include a list of attributes of the transaction related to be used as a key when referencing the master relation, which key is assumed to be the same number of attributes from the left of the relation. Necessary variations on POST include POST to accumulate (POST-Add and POST-SUB) and POST to replace (POST-REP for a latest date or status, etc.)

For example, a relation of cheque transactions might exist:

Relation TR (name, cheque-amount)

PHIL	50
PHIL	75
SUE	20
JAMES	10

The operation EDIT TR TO AO WITH NAME results in the transaction of JAMES being flagged as a transaction without a record in the master relation AO. The operation POST TR TO AO WITH NAME results in the updated relation:

Relation AO (name, bank-balance, sex)

PHIL	87	M
JACK	118	M
SUE	291	F

The EDIT operator would, of course, be unnecessary if the DBMS used could do automatic referential integrity checking. The POST operator is a desirable addition to standard relational algebra as it can effect the bulk of file-updating functions required in business data processing systems.

Transaction processing extensions

Batch processing has certain desirable characteristics from the accounting point of view – a natural auditability and ease of control. However, 'transaction processing', wherein the edit and post cycle is completed for each single transaction (rather than for whole batches), is often preferred. This mode of processing transactions tends to use more of the computer resources but may be more efficient for the operator, as less paper shuffling is involved in correcting errors.

A TRANPRO operator for transaction processing may be implemented to make use of information supplied in the database schema. Such an augmented definition of a transaction record for WITHDRAWALS might appear:

attribute notations

--- ---

ACCOUNT-NUMBER	XREF	ACCOUNT-MASTER, ACCOUNT-NUMBER
	LKUP	ACCOUNT-NAME
AMOUNT	POST-SUB	BALANCE
DATE	POST-REP	DATE-LAST-TRANSACTION

This record has three fields: an account number, an amount, and a date. The notation on the account number field means that the account number is to be validated against the ACCOUNT-NUMBER field (which must be a key) in the ACCOUNT-MASTER relation. The ACCOUNT-NAME field from the previously referenced file, ACCOUNT-MASTER, is to be displayed for visual verification. The amount field is to be posted by subtracting from the BALANCE field in the previously referenced file, ACCOUNT-MASTER. The date is to be posted by replacement to the DATE-LAST-TRANSACTION field.

Since the detailed information necessary for the operation is carried in the schema, this transaction processing operation is invoked with the command TRANPRO WITHDRAWALS. TRANPRO results in a screen-oriented processing of transactions, one transaction per screen. Visual validation of data and correction is allowed in a standardised manner.

'Ledger-card-model' extensions

The EDIT and POST operators support a batch mode of processing transactions. The TRANPRO supports a transaction processing style of transaction handling in a screen-oriented manner with one transaction per screen. As an alternative to support interactive processing of transactions in a screen-oriented manner, a 'ledger-card' operator and model may be used. The parameters to the LEDGER operator can be a master relation name and a historical transaction relation name. The result of entering the LEDGER command is a transformation of the screen into a ledger card image. In traditional accounting, ledger-card fashion, header information from the master relation is displayed at the top upon entry of the key attribute values for the master relation. At the same time transactions from the transaction relation are displayed in a list as detail entries down the ledger card image. The detailed information necessary to carry out the processing is obtained from the schema as in TRANPRO.

For example, the operation LEDGER AO WITH TR and the entry of the key value 'JACK' results in a screen image:

```
------------------------------------------------------
NAME        JACK      BALANCE    87      ACCOUNT-TYPE DEPOSIT
                      CHEQUE AMOUNT
                          50
                          75
------------------------------------------------------
```

A new transaction may be entered at the bottom of the list of old transactions. The new transaction is POSTed automatically with LEDGER, changing the BALANCE field above as the return key is processed at the end of the entry of the new transaction.

Calculations and report writing

Arithmetic operations are supported by the column operators ADD, SUBTRACT, MULTIPLY, and DIVIDE. This type of capability is common in database application systems.[14] In addition, the system can provide a ZERO operator to re-set period accumulating balances at the end of the period. Its arguments are a relation name and an attribute name.

It is an objective of current research to integrate a spreadsheet facility into this relational-algebra-based set of end-user programming components.[15] This will provide the user with the ability to model and to produce more elaborate report formats. (The spreadsheet is the most successful end-user tool developed to date, and the use of it in an end-user applications development system is desirable.)

10.5   A MENU-INTERPRETER

A facility for accessing these relational operators and compound procedures of the operators via a menu is provided with an operator MENU. MENU takes as its argument the name of a relation which contains other operators and their arguments ordered and named according to the work flow desired. Such a relation might appear:

Relation PR (menu name, description, statement)

DAILY	key trans.	MAINTAIN TRANS
DAILY	edit trans.	EDIT TR TO AO WITH NAME
DAILY	post trans.	POST TR TO AO WITH NAME
MONTHLY	key adjs.	MAINTAIN ADJ

The statement MENU PR would result in a first menu screen:

```
------------------
      MAIN MENU
      1.  DAILY
      2.  MONTHLY
  Your Selection _____
------------------
```

A selection of '1' would bring up the DAILY menu with the selections of key, edit, or post transactions as specified in the PR relation. Such a menu-generation facility is available with many application-oriented operating environments developed by commercial vendors. Menus are often preferred to command language by managers and accountants.

10.6   TOWARD THE EXECUTABLE APPLICATION SCHEMA

Data processing systems have transaction files which are processed to update master files. If the database schema is augmented with denotations for cross-reference (XREF), lookup (LKUP) and posting (POST) as described in the transaction processing discussion above, it is straightforward for a generator program to determine which file definitions are for master files and which are for transaction files. Appropriate menus can be generated automatically for processing the transaction files against the master files if the time cycles for generation of the transactions are also specified. If one of 'daily, weekly, monthly, yearly' is appended to the transaction files in the schema, menus can be generated complete with operation specifications for typical simple business date processing systems. Even some report generation (monthly listings of the master files in order by key, for example) can be generated according to a convention.

Rather than using a generator program to provide this capability, the augmented schema could be executed directly by an interpreter. This is a realisation of a true 'executable application schema'. As the database schema separates the logical from the physical for the data files, such an application schema can separate the declarative from the procedural specifications for an application. The application schema contains a declarative specification for the system. Procedures are derived from conventions embedded in the schema interpreter program.

In the executable schema approach, the manager or the accountant need only define the information inputs and outputs desired from the system. The system executes this definition directly with no requirement for 'programming'.

10.7   USER-FACILITY ARCHITECTURE

The end-user application development tools described above could be embedded in a user-facility which translates the tool requirements into the language of the host DBMS. This user-facility could be personal-computer-based. This would allow the functioning of the tool-based applications to be supported by standard high-level update and retrieval facilities of a DBMS. The DBMS would not need to know of the presence of the toolset. Host-language coding to access the DBMS could be avoided in many cases. If this interface were properly table-based, the user-facility could be a gateway to several DBMSs. In fact, the end-user could access several DBMSs and even several central computer installations without being aware of it. The user's functioning would be at the toolset level with the DBMS accessing taken care of by his personal-computer-based user-facility.

This means the manager or accountant can define his systems using the methods outlined above and then execute them on any available computer without learning the details of that computer. This would achieve true application systems portability.

10.8 SUMMARY AND CONCLUSION

The foregoing reviews the relational algebra approach to data manipulation languages and the relational data model. It is shown how a minor redefinition of a standard operator can give an EDIT operator and how a POST operator, which is certainly no more complex than other standard relational algebra operators, can be created. Also, a 'transaction processing' operator and a 'ledger-card-model', for accountants interactive, screen-oriented transaction processing are presented. A menu-interpretation facility is described along with other database features which would be useful in an end-user applications development environment for managers and accountants. The relational algebra with these extensions is proposed as an end-user programming facility for management and accounting processing.

The advantages of letting the manager or accountant implement systems directly in this manner are quick and economical development, and ease of training (from the use of standard and familiar facilities and from the fact that the end-user designed the system). The disadvantages are the usual ones of using high-level facilities – possibly poor performance and standards rather than custom functions. The overcoming of these same disadvantages through improved techniques and user education has been the trend in computer use until now, and this will no doubt continue into the future.

References

1. McLean, E. R. 'End Users as Application Developers' *MIS Quarterly*, December 1979.
2. Berrisford, T., and Wetherbe, J. 'Heuristic Development: A Redesign of Systems Design' *MIS Quarterly* , March, 1979.
3. Schlueter, L. *User-designed Computing* (Lexington Books, 1982).
4. Zloof, M. M. 'Query-by-Example: A Data Base Language' IBM *Systems Journal*, Vol. 16, No. 4, 1977.
5. Hammer, M. *et al.*, 'A Very High Level Programming Language for Data Processing Applications' *Communications of the ACM*, November, 1977.
6. Watanabe, T., *et al.*, 'A Simple Database Language for Personal Computers' *Communications of the ACM*, September, 1983.

7. Codd, E. F. 'A Relational Model of Data for Large Shared Data Banks' *Communications of the ACM*, June, 1970.
8. Tsichritzis, D. C. and Lochovsky, F. H. *Data base Management Systems* (Academic Press, 1977).
9. Martin, J. *End-user's Guide to Database* (Prentice-Hall, 1982).
10. Wiederhold, G. *Database Design* (McGraw-Hill, 1983).
11. Weiderhold, *ibid*.
12. Date, C. J. *An Introduction to Data Base Systems* (Addison-Wesley, 1981).
13. Benbasat, I., and Wand, Y. 'A Dialogue Generator and Its Use in DSS Design' *Information and Management* September, 1982.
14. Orman, L. 'A Familial Specification Language for Database Application Systems' *Computing Languages*, Vol. 8, No. 3, 1983.
15. Merrett, T. H. *Relational Information Systems* (Reston, 1984).

11 Looking Forward

Richard L. Shell

11.1 INTRODUCTION

Overview

The purpose of this chapter is to briefly review the recent past, and project some of the changes that are likely to impact computers and their applications. Four major areas are discussed: computer hardware, software, information systems and computer applications, and human resource considerations. In future computerised systems, considerable change will occur in the way data is received and utilised.

Research is presently being undertaken to determine the future requirements of computer systems in manufacturing as well as the service industries. Several hardware and software improvement targets have been identified. Examples of improvements include improved parallel processing architecture, real time simulation programming techniques, faster CPU access, expanded networking capabilities, and voice input/output. The developments associated with operating system improvements, data base design, and artificial intelligence are also high priorities for future computer systems.

The continuing implementation of factory and office automation, and the changes taking place throughout the world in information technologies has created new human training requirements. The skill level of future workers associated with these fields will need to increase. Familiarisation with computers will be necessary for the majority of workers in the future.

Resistance to computerisation

The major barriers to widespread computer usage are programming concerns and economic limitations. For example, even in technologically advanced nations only about 1 per cent of the population know how to program. The development of less detailed programming languages will ease this somewhat; however, this is still a concern. Options include query-type systems where communication takes

Figure 11.1 Microchip development

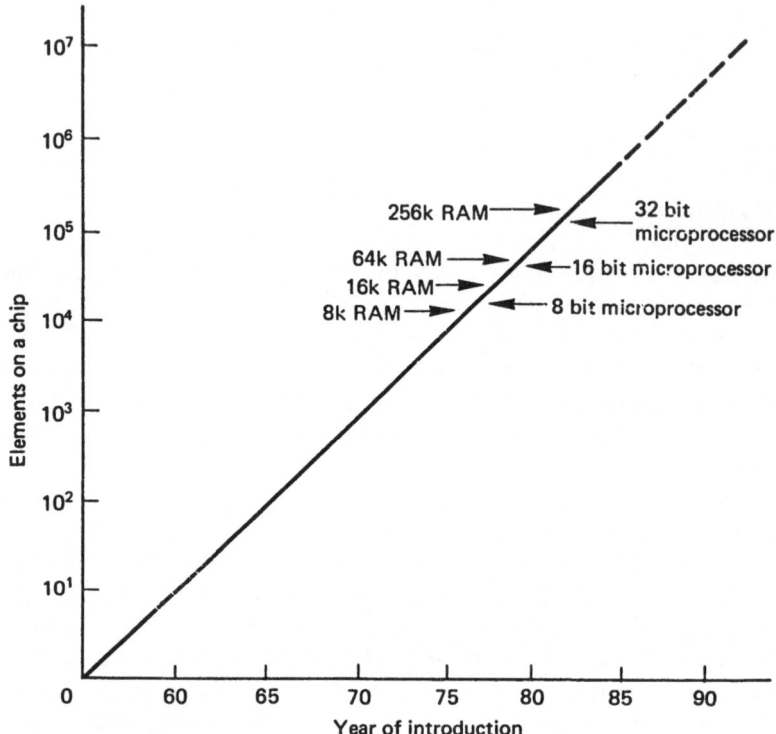

place without prior programming experience, modular language where pre-programmed modules for separate functions are linked together, and natural language (though limited in potential now holds promise for the future). The computer environment itself is foreign to most users, with unfamiliar symbols and technical terms required for computer system development.

The economic barrier to computerisation has at this time been greatly reduced and will be lessened through continued microchip development. Miniaturisation has permitted logarithmic gains in the development of memory and processor capacity (reference Figure 11.1). The reduction in cost of micro chips continues to follow technical advances in the design and manufacture of microelectronics.

The computer industry

Worldwide, the computer industry is rapidly developing. The top 100 data processing companies in the US had total sales revenues of $91.8 billion in 1983, up 18 per cent over the 1982 total of $77.8 billion. The market for data processing can be divided into four major equipment segments; mainframe, mini, micro, and office systems. An approximate breakdown of total 1983 US revenues and their average percentage rate of increase over 1982 is shown below.

Data processing category	Percent of total revenue	Percent annual increase
Mainframe	41	8
Mini	30	15
Micro	17	74
Office Systems	12	21

Revenues for the total US data processing industry are projected to increase nearly 20 percent annually with 1986 revenues exceeding $150 billion (reference Figure 11.2). Growth rates are anticipated to remain about the same for mainframes and office systems. Mini sales may slightly decline, while micro revenue growth is expected to sharply increase.

11.2 COMPUTER HARDWARE IN THE FUTURE

Introduction

Future computer systems will move from sequential centralised systems to newer generations of parallel, decentralised systems, in which a number of subsystems will work together. Processing is becoming less concerned with numerical calculations. Tomorrow's users will have a need for handling larger quantities of non-numeric data, such as images, graphics, sentences, and speech. The key to the development of future generations of computers will be the software systems that support the hardware operations and applications.

Figure 11.2   The US computer industry sales for the top 100 companies

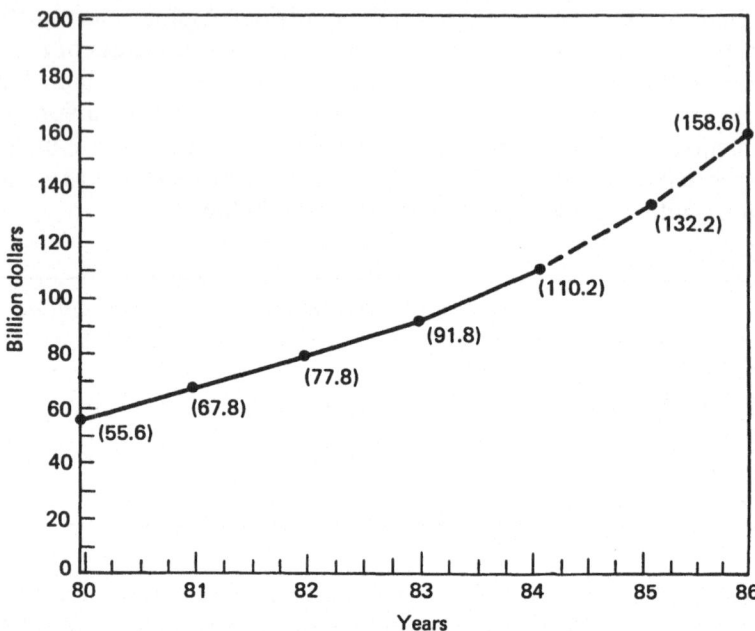

Software issues will be critical to future generations of machines, not just because they are essential to the idea of computing itself, but because they are less well understood than the parallel computer architectures which are being developed today.

The next generation of machines will be based on developments in three principal areas. The first of these is the further development of artificial intelligence (AI). A central theme of AI is the development of expert systems. Research in this area is based on the construction of programs which are comparable in both functionality and efficiency with the best human experts. The second area is parallel computing. Single processor systems have reached a limit at which further improvements in circuit technology are not feasible. Today's cycle times in uniprocessor systems are more than half used by propagation delays between active devices. Consequently, the advent of parallel computing is a necessity in future generation machines. The third area is the development of very-large scale integration (VLSI) circuit technology. Technology themes supporting breakthroughs in micro-electronics will include the further development of gallium arsenide integrated circuits (IC's) and the development of VLSI computer aided design (CAD) systems which will automate the design of other electronic devices.

Parallel computing

Future computers will be required to operate at much higher rates of speed than can be achieved on today's sequential machines. Uniprocessor machines have reached a limit in their operating speeds at approximately one nanosecond. Further technological improvements can expect to improve this by at best, one order of magnitude (Cotellessa, 1983). For these reasons, the next generation of computers will be parallel machines which allow the computer to perform many tasks concurrently. Until now parallel systems were largely ignored because speed improvements were always available on single processor machines.

The idea of parallel computing transcends hardware and is a total systems issue. Parallel architectures have been developed during recent years. However, problems exist in the development of parallel software, parallel memory, and I/O devices for parallel architectures. Another important design issue that must be addressed is the cooperation which must exist between parallel processors. Individual processors must work together in the areas of control, communication, and programming. Current research projects have usually concentrated only in a single area (memory, parallel software, etc.) which will be needed as part of an overall system. Consequently, parallel computer systems will not be realisable until all parallel processing problems have been solved (Davis, 1983).

VLSI technology

Today's engineers and scientists better understand the concept of VLSI technology than either AI or parallel computing. VLSI technology is critical to the development of future generation machines, as it will be a necessary link in future integrated systems.

One area of VLSI research is gallium arsenide integrated circuits. Gallium arsenide dissipates approximately the same amount of power as silicon, however its switching speeds are ten times faster (Eden, Livingston and Welch, 1983). When fully developed, gallium arsenide IC's will permit the design of higher speed logic and memory circuits.

Another area of VLSI research is the development of CAD systems. VLSI devices are very complex in nature and their designs require some automation. Research is under way in the US and other countries to combine large-scale parallel processors with CAD and expert systems to support VLSI design (Cotellessa, 1983). Japan's goal is to build fifth generation machines from chips containing the equivalent of more than one-million transistors. For this to be accomplished, automated integration techniques will have to be developed (Waltz, 1983).

Mainframe computers

For the past several years mainframe developments have received less press because of the interest in micros. However, the importance and need for the mainframe for certain applications in the future remains strong.

Presently, it has been estimated that about 50 million dollars are spent annually in the US for research on very high performance computers and related software. By contrast, Japan's centrally coordinated effort spends about $200 million annually from both government and industry and is aimed at increasing super computer capacity by the order of three magnitudes before 1990.

A major direction of mainframe research is to build a parallel processing computer. A 64 to 100 processor machine is possible very soon. Ultimately, a machine with tens of thousands of processors is possible. Most computer architects see parallel processing (the simultaneous use of more than one processor on different parts of the same task) as the only route to the super-computers of tomorrow.

The future mainframe computers will incorporate many ideas from the field of artificial intelligence. Future computers will be much more human-like, using stored reservoirs of knowledge to make expert judgements and decisions. Building these 'thinking' machines will require radical changes in computer design and software. Future machines will process non-numerical information such as pictures and graphs. Knowledge processors will be built, not data processors. The computer will understand normal speech. By 1990, the Japanese expect computer vocabularies to top 10 000 words and be as easy to use as the telephone (Martin and Shell, 1980). These machines will serve as intelligent assistants, giving users access to a broad range of information and expertise.

The Japanese plan is to develop the mainframe computer in three stages leading to a prototype by 1990. They are hoping that foreign companies and other countries will join the project as it progresses. Some Japanese industry executives still see the project as too grandiose and futuristic. Officials in charge of the fifth generation project concede that it could take longer than expected. Some predict that project goals will not be attained until the year 2000 (Martin and Shell, 1980).

More mainframe manufacturers are moving toward building machines that are fault-tolerant. A society in the throes of computerisation is strongly drawn to machines that keep running despite part failures. The secret of fault-tolerance is not failure proof parts or the ability to repair themselves, but simply incorporating a large number of redundant components.

Fault-tolerant systems have been available since the mid-1970s when Tandem Computers (US) shipped their first 'Non-Stop System'. As the cost of employing people continues to rise, day-to-day business operations have been entrusted to computers in ever greater quantities. Therefore, the cost of a system failure has also risen and boosted the demand for fault tolerance. Simultaneously, declining hardware costs have made commercially fault-tolerant systems more affordable. IBM Corporation's first fault-tolerant system was a networked configuration of Series/1 computers. DEC's early system was an interconnect structure for sharing of processor and storage resources. The five principal characteristics of present day fault-tolerant computing systems are redundancy, failure detection, diagnosis, repair and software recovery after a failure. In the future, fault-tolerant computers will even further penetrate the market as hardware costs drop and the dependance on computerised information rises.

Because of their history, most people think of a computer as an electrical device. The operations carried out by a computer are logical and arithmetic; and could be done by any of several means. The potential exists for constructing a computer device in which signals are transmitted by beams of laser radiation rather than electric currents. The optical computer may be capable of trillions of operations per second.

The speed of the computer in its calculations is dependent on the length of time it takes for a switch to change states, among other factors. Even the fastest transistors presently in use cannot be made to change states in less than about a nanosecond. An optical device analogous to the transistor could switch from one transmission state to another in about a picosecond. The optical 'transistor' could be employed to build computers that would process information in much the same way as an electronic machine but much faster. In the more distant future the capabilities of the optical transistor could transform the organisation of the computer itself. Each optical 'transistor' could be the site of simultaneous switching operations; in contrast an electronic transistor of the kind employed in a computer has only two output stages. The adoption of devices with more than two stable states could lead to a new system of computer logic.

The course of supercomputer mainframe development in the future is one of much uncertainty. The future will certainly hold an increase in failure-proof computer systems, as business depends more and more on computers for daily operations. As the development of the new mainframes occurs there will be many delays and problems. The mainframes are susceptible to these difficulties more than other computer equipment because they have typically been at the leading edge of technology. Combating these problems successfully will lead to larger, faster and more intelligent mainframes.

Micro and minicomputers

Marketing of computers costing less than $100 000 (US) into small and medium size businesses will surge in this decade. It has been estimated that sales of business computers will nearly triple during the 1980s. According to recent marketing studies, nearly four million small business computers will be sold during the late 1980s. Even more startling, 75 per cent of these will be computer systems that cost less than $10 000 (US). During the 1980s some $52 billion, cumulatively, will be expended by small businesses on computer systems in the US. Of that, $35 billion will be spent on hardware and systems software; $17 billion on applications software. All this anticipated market growth will be filled by a variety of micro and minicomputers. Most forecasting is extremely hazardous and at best is only moderately accurate. This is especially true for microcomputer technology because of its rapid development and change.

Perhaps the most important area of new computer technologies is in microprocessor design and production. Microprocessor cost, speed, power, reliability and word length will be very dynamic areas of future change. However, predicting precisely what type of changes will occur would be extremely difficult. Storage devices for this equipment will strive for denser storage, quicker access and lower cost.

Portability will continue to be a high priority for microcomputer development. The present limit of size reduction is governed by a viewing screen suitable to human sight and a keyboard to fit human hand/finger size. Both of these limitations may be eliminated with voice recognition for input and optical projection and audio for output. A variety of portable micros are presently available and more are likely to appear in the future.

The best indicator of future growth and development of 'smaller' computers may be a projection from the first three years following IBM's entry into the microcomputer marketplace. During mid 1981, IBM released the PC. The top three sales leaders in the microcomputer industry at that time were Apple Computer, Commodore, and Tandy Corporation (Radio Shack). By the end of 1982, IBM had annual sales of $500 million and ranked second in the market between Apple Computer ($664 million) and Tandy Corporation ($466 million). Commodore had dropped to fourth place with sales of $368 million. By the end of 1983, IBM clearly moved to number one in the micro market with over a five-fold increase in sales ($2600 million). Apple fell to number two with sales of $1085 million, with Commodore ($927 million) and Tandy Corp. ($598 million) in the third and fourth positions.

At the present time, IBM continues to dominate the microcomputer industry. Its release of the PC AT in 1984 establishes future direction. The PC AT uses the Intel 80286 microprocessor, a 16/24 bit machine, a considerable advance over the earlier PC and PC XT models that utilised the Intel 8088 8/16 bit microprocessor. The PC AT supports networking, has internal user memory ranging from 256 KB to 3 MB, has two high-speed disk drives each containing 20 MB of data storage, and uses either DOS or XENIX operating systems.

The future developments of super microcomputers will include larger networking capabilities, expanded user memory, and much larger random access data storage devices. In short, exceeding the capabilities and capacities of present day minicomputers. Computer classifications in the future will likely be reduced to large mainframes and small micro-mini's.

Cost trends

The cost of acquiring a computer system decreases between two and three times every five years, and memory costs have decreased ten times during the past five years. This is due largely to new technologies like large-scale integration (LSI) memories, and improved disk storage devices. Design improvements and the stack-ability of disk drives will maintain these cost advantages over semiconductor memory for the next several years. With microprocessor cost decreasing at a faster rate than whole systems, the tendency will be to build multiprocessors capable of separate functions on the same physical computer board. Power supplies and packaging account for about 30 per cent of the system and hold promise for further cost reduction with higher-volume manufacturing methods. The $1.00 (US) per watt cost standard is slowly decreasing and LSI will provide future cost reductions. For example, an LSI version of DEC's PDP-8 can run on flashlight batteries. Integration in the packaging and component enclosure may be achieved by introducing processors and storage area into the terminal's cabinet.

Operating costs for computer systems typically exceed initial acquisition costs, but are spread over several years and are therefore less noticeable. Programming is usually the largest operating cost. For example, though the sources are not really comparable, the five cent byte of memory can cost as much as a dollar to fill with software, and this ratio is projected to go as high as 1000 to 1 in the future. Trends will be to reduce the investment in training users by incorporating self-teaching and/or prepackaged software to each unit. Another operating cost that is increasing is field service and maintenance. This can amount to 50 per cent of the purchase price for a small to medium sized computer. Other labour costs include operators, often with the sole purpose of data entry. Another cost that is sizable over a computer's lifetime is electricity. Inefficient power supplies can add 20 to 30 per cent to operating costs, and 10 per cent more for ventilation and cooling. Low power semiconductors will be commonly utilised in the future to reduce this cost. Expenditures for miscellaneous supplies are another cost of operating that can be fairly substantial. For example, printers for larger systems often consume a million sheets of paper a month, and a diskette-drive micro system costing a few thousand dollars may require 20 diskette-packs at $250.00 each over its lifetime, or approximately the initial cost of the

Figure 11.3　Software complexity

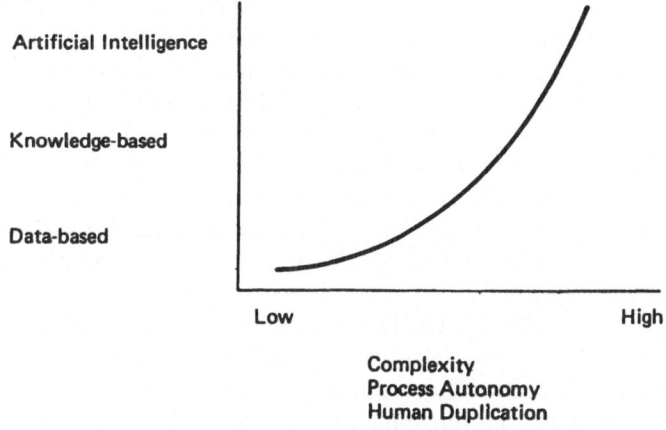

Complexity
Process Autonomy
Human Duplication

unit. A design trend to reduce these costs will be toward non-removable storage media and additional display devices.

11.3　COMPUTER SOFTWARE IN THE FUTURE

Introduction

Can a computer system of the future duplicate the functions and complexities of the human brain? To accomplish this, the advancements needed in hardware and software are beyond the comprehension of most people. Yet, what was computed on the largest vacuum tube computers of 30 years ago can be accomplished today on a hand held microcomputer. To better understand the requirement for a human thinking computer system, it is helpful to review the earlier years of software design of data-based systems through knowledge-based systems to artificial intelligence systems. Figure 11.3 shows the varying degrees of complexity, process autonomy, and need for human duplication during completion of task, and the level to which the software duplicates the human process.

One of the first areas of computer programming was to solve problems in mathematics. Logic and operations were well defined; computers could grind out solutions to simple problems. Glorified

electrical adding machines typified the state of the art until technological advances allowed mass storage of data. This signified the
beginning of true data-based systems. Today, almost all computers
outside the realm of research are considered data-based systems.
Software programs convert data into meaningful information for the
end user. Presently, commercially available software allows the user
to establish archives, make as many lists as imaginable, type letters,
prepare budgets, keep track of accounts, read about far-away places,
communicate with other computers, perform complex mathematical
calculations, or play games. In the future, the computer will become
even more versatile, and serve all of the user's computational and
informational needs.

In the early 1980s the US Department of Defense (DOD) had 58
different computer models from 29 different manufacturers that
constituted 250 different computer systems which used 43 different
control languages. To alleviate this problem, the DOD decided to
develop a high-level language called Ada. This language is machine
independent. Programs will run on any machine with only slight
modification. Also, programming errors are identified in greater
detail to assist the debugging process of new programs.

In microcomputers, the Apple Corporation Lisa (Logical Integrated Software Architecture) is an excellent example of a commercially available user friendly software system. Typically, a person
needs at least 20 to 40 hours to master a personal computer. With
Lisa, it takes about 20 minutes because there is no need to understand programming. The user works on documents. All this is accomplished through the use of pictures and a small hand control
(mouse) to locate screen displays.

Expert systems

An expert system is composed of two basic parts. One is the collection of information that experts in the field use to make decisions.
This forms the data base. The second part is the set of values that
experts apply to the data. These are called inferences or rules. To
obtain information for the development of an expert system, someone has to interview an expert on the subject and get them to explain
their reasoning behind their judgements. As of yet, there are only a
few functioning expert systems.

One of the earlier systems was developed at Stanford University
for the University of Pittsburgh Medical Center. Caduceus is a

program that can diagnose 550 out of 700 or so diseases in the field of internal medicine. The attending physician inputs preliminary data such as pulse rate, blood pressure, and temperature. The program will then ask questions for the physician to answer. Through this series of questions and answers, the program will submit a diagnosis. The diagnosis is correct over 90 per cent of the time. Another system was developed by John McDermot at Carnegie-Mellon University, for Digital Equipment Corporation (DEC). The system, labeled R1, started out as a 250 inference (rules applied to data) program. Since its inception, the program has grown to 1200 rules that integrated 1000 different components into the VAX system. DEC more recently worked on XSEL, a program that allows a computer salesperson to operate a computer terminal and provide a potential customer a list of components needed for a specific system. Other recent programs include:

Prospect a geological program to help detect mineral deposits
GEL determines sequences of nucleic acids in molecular biology
Genesis simulates cloning experiments, and IBM's version of computer self-diagnostics.

Expert systems do not come cheaply. It has been estimated that for any program containing more than 50 rules, one interviewer can get one finished product rule out of one expert in one hour. For a full-fledged program of 500 rules, development would require at least 5 person-years. In addition to sophisticated software, hardware must improve to obtain a true knowledge-based system. To make one inference, a computer usually requires 100 to 1000 steps. A true knowledge-based system needs to handle 100 000 to one million logical inferences per second (lips). Today's hardware can handle about 10 000 lips.

With knowledge-based systems in their infancy, how far away is artificial intelligence? There is a long way to go before research results can be translated into practical systems. What are the problems? A recent article in *Personal Computing* (Dean, 1983) summarised the following:

What seems to be the key distinction is that computers operate on algorithms and people operate on heuristics. An algorithm is a mechanism which is known to work, and is guaranteed to give you a right answer every time. A heuristic is a general rule which isn't guaranteed to work, but it might, and is a good way to go about trying to do it. The idea behind heuristics is that you're willing to give up complete accuracy as long as you get the common cases right most of the time.

To create true artificial intelligence, more research of the human mind is needed in such areas as knowledge organisation, how people make inferences and hypotheses of new situations, and mental processing/work output (Shell and Okogbaa, 1983).

Artificial intelligence

The building blocks of artificial intelligence include: knowledge-based (expert) systems, natural language processing, speech recognition, and computer vision. Future intelligent systems will have the following characteristics: the ability to learn from experience, the ability to act on natural language input, perception, and the ability to assess given situations.

Knowledge-based systems use computer programs to reason from a limited domain of knowledge. In this sense computer programs can approach and sometimes exceed human performance. These expert systems will be modular in nature with a clear separation between the knowledge base, the input data, and the methods for applying the general knowledge to the problem. Consequently, program modifications can be made by changing only the knowledge base whereas in conventional computer programs the knowledge and the methods for applying the knowledge are intermixed which makes alterations more difficult. As previously stated, while a few useful programs are in use, expert system technology is still at an early stage.

A major focus of research in AI is to develop computers that can communicate with humans in natural language. Society is becoming increasingly dependent on the generation and distribution of information. Therefore, information technology will be greatly enhanced by the advent of natural language machines. Natural language processing will enable computers to interact with that portion of the population that is unable or unwilling to learn formal computing. Having a machine that can interact with humans on a one-to-one basis is not yet a reality. However, considerable research has been done during recent years to confirm its feasibility.

Many application areas exist for future natural language machines. Two of these areas are in document understanding and document generation. Document understanding involves documents which are read by a machine and then arranged into larger frameworks of knowledge. With this knowledge, the machine will alert people who need this information (usually some small part of the total) and then answer questions on its text. This type of system will be useful in distributing information to particular levels of management as part of an overall intelligent network. Document generation involves the idea of translating information stored in a formal computer language into a natural language (Waltz, 1983). In this sense, computers will be able to generate documents in a variety of natural languages for different readers. This will be particularly valuable to developing countries wanting to import technology and information from industrial nations (Shell and Damachi, 1983).

The concepts of speech recognition and computer vision are still in their primitive stages. Progress in speech recognition is being somewhat delayed by a lack of acoustic devices for recognizing continuous speech (Cotellessa, 1983). The best computer vision systems are able to locate objects only under limited conditions. Developing a computer system with general purpose sight is still well into the future (Kanade and Reddy, 1983).

Trends

There are a few general overriding trends in the software field. One is the drive towards standardisation. With the proliferation of computers into society, both at home and the work place, a truly efficient system requires software that is capable of operating on several different computer systems. Also, standard programming will decrease the amount of personnel needed to adapt, document, maintain, and program software for different systems.

Another area of concern is the rising cost of personnel to staff the computer system. The largest cost of a computing system is for secretaries, managers, and engineers that use the system. With this in mind, software is being designed to be more 'user friendly' and help the operator obtain the information in the correct form for immediate use. To achieve this, software is moving toward more application-oriented programming than general purpose programming that is adapted to any situation. Also, software that has reached a high level of standardisation and stability is designed into a package such as a programmable read only memory chip (PROM) or an erasable PROM. This helps reduce costs because this type of hardware can be produced at a much lower cost than software.

The overall cost for software is expected to drop in the future. It is estimated that the relative cost of sensing and control computer systems software will decrease by 50 per cent by the year 2000.

11.4 INFORMATION SYSTEMS AND COMPUTER APPLICATIONS IN THE FUTURE

Management information systems

The management information system (MIS) of the future will be a logical plan linking various parts together to form a unity whole. The two key phrases in this statement are logical plan and to form a unity.

Most management information systems of today evolved (or are evolving) from completely independent functions. For example, Engineering had their own system as did Production and Inventory Control, and Purchasing. Each system operated independently of the others, with some duplication of services and overlapping data bases. Confusion and complications mounted with the varying systems. To control this increasing bureaucracy and cost, systems more recently have been integrated into a unified MIS.

The future MIS will involve the logical plan to distribute information pertinent to several areas such as Manufacturing, Purchasing, Sales, and Scheduling from a common base of data and knowledge. The MIS will draw information from sources such as marketing information, corporate resource plans, operations plans, and corporate strategies. All the information that is generated by the corporation can be organised and distributed to support management decisions (Martin and Shell, 1980).

An example to illustrate a future MIS would involve a corporation using just-in-time delivery for production. During daily operations on the automatic inspection line, a vital part starts to be rejected constantly. This information is automatically entered into daily rejection reports. Due to an automatic notification for high scrap rates, this information is distributed to various areas. Manufacturing is notified that there is a problem with a vital part. Engineering is given the specifications of the rejected part for investigation. Purchasing receives information to contact suppliers for more parts to cover the amount rejected. Sales receives notification that assemblies requiring these parts will be delayed and to contact the customer. Management is also aware of the problem and can keep a close watch for further developments. All of this was done through the use of a comprehensive management information system.

Overview of computer applications

The next generation of computers and information systems will find a variety of applications. These computers will upgrade information technology in the areas of industrial automation, office automation, and in the retailing and service industries (Shell, 1982). All users of computers, including systems analysts and computer engineers, will be greatly affected by future generation machines. Each of these applications is feasible today on the basis of technology which has been demonstrated in research settings. Advances in integrated information-management systems, computer architectures, and human-machine interfaces are required for these applications to become realisable.

The past several years have seen a vast increase in the number of robots and CAD/CAM systems in use in industrial settings. Future factories will also see increased applications in inventory management, product-cost estimating, and in expert systems for design uses. The components necessary to implement these ideas include software systems which will be vital in tying together the information related to design and manufacturing. Available also, will be libraries of modular robot control routines. This will enable robots to be used in low-volume production settings (Douglas, 1983).

Technology has been devised which will completely handle the management of office information. This technology will next be brought together in systems for implementation in office settings. The next generation components which will make this a reality include powerful database software for management. As previously mentioned, users will have systems available to them which employ human-machine interactions through voice commands, voice output, and natural language processing. Expert systems will be available to assist in applying computer systems and also for helping retrieve information relevant to the user. Communication in the office will be enhanced by systems which link together telephone lines and office computers through Local Area Networks (LANs). This will also open the door for long distance communications which will include electronic mail and phone message systems.

A great abundance of applications in information service industries are awaiting the new generation of computers. Expert systems could be utilised in several areas, including searching of property and court records, tax and financial planning, and analysis and information systems for use in repairing such things as cars and appliances. Hardware and software systems, which have been in existence, must be integrated together for these ideas to become effective. Attention must also be paid to the development of more natural interface systems which will allow easier access to available information (Douglas, 1983).

The development of future computers will see an increase in the automation of the computer industry itself. The computers being developed today will be doing much of the design work on the generation of machines that follow them. Hardware and software is being developed to semi-automate program design and for use in debugging and maintaining programs. Expert systems will also be used for the fault diagnosis of computer hardware. The ultimate computer of tomorrow will be a machine which will completely maintain itself and even, on its own, design a machine to take its place.

Information systems and manufacturing

The future of information systems for use within a manufacturing facility is a topic which is rapidly changing with technology. In industrialised countries, the labour force is changing from goods producing, hard manufacturing to information-oriented software production. As this takes place, the need for high quality and understandable information will increase. The changes being made in the technology and sciences of manufacturing are leading to automated factories (factories of the future) run by a multitude of machines with minimal human interface (Shell, 1982).

These factories of the future are essential if a country is going to develop a strong manufacturing base and be able to compete in the world marketplace. To analyse the information needs of automated factories of the future one must be familiar with the basic types of information inputs which will be available.

The anatomy and thought processes of humans are being incorporated in the next generation of robotics and automated machines. A comparison of the human body to advanced technologies is given below:

bones	robot arm or other automated equipment elements
brain	microprocessor/computer

consciousness program execution/operation, real-time processing
feet guidance systems, obstacle recognition, support devices
hearing audio input, language understanding
joints hinge or universal joint
judgement logic circuits, decision making
knowledge data, expert systems, artificial intelligence
learning data input, pattern recognition and interpretation
memory storage devices
nerves electronics, conductors, semiconductors
reasoning heuristic trials, deductive processes
sight vision and image processing
skeleton machine structure
speech audio output, voice synthesis

Currently, there are appoximately five to six thousand robots in use in the United States, with the population anticipated to increase to over one hundred thousand by the year 1990 (Cotellessa 1983). Industrial robots can provide continuous production at lower costs. Combined with the new technology of vision systems, tactile sensing, sonar, object recognition, and computers the robot will become more advanced (intelligent) and more useful.

In addition to advanced information systems, the future will also see advances in factory equipment. While most development will be in computer architecture and processing techniques, there will be many developments in machine tools and process control equipment. An important need is the development of a secure data storage device for use on machine tools and factory equipment. Japanese tool makers currently use magnetic bubble memory devices, which are built into the machine controls. However, these devices may not be reliable in metal manufacturing operations due to possible magnetic interference. As manufacturing techniques become more automated and complex, larger and more secure memory devices will be incorporated in most factory equipment.

Information use in factory operations

The fundamental information needs of the future factory will basically remain the same. Factory managers will still need to know performance indicators, manufacturing information; such as tooling data, machine operation, maintenance, cost data, power consumption, downtime, and general management information involving all operating functions. For the actual manufacturing shop floor there will be a need for interpretation of such data so that it may be appropriately applied. Interestingly, this is how data is used in manufacturing today. There will, however, be a major difference; the interpretors, no longer human, but machines such as industrial robots, microprocessors, object recognition devices, and a multitude of other high-tech devices.

The transfer of information will occur as a series of binary numbers, generated by electrical (or optical) pulses. One such example of this can be seen at the Mazak Machine Tool Corporation in Florence, Kentucky (USA). A small scale factory of the future, Mazak utilises a binary code on part pallets, which is in turn interpreted by the machine tool for part processing data, tool selection, and inventory/work in process control. The central factory computer tracks this data and generates reports for management, in addition to performing actual machine control. While not entirely automated, Mazak serves as a current example of a manufacturing firm applying advanced technology.

While all computers operate in a similar machine code, there has been a proliferation of computer operating systems and languages. As the application of computer factory control increases so does the need for standardisation of a factory programming language. One which is easily understandable to programmers and operators is natural language. This is needed so that robots, machine tools, material handling, and object recognition or inspection devices can operate in harmony. There is also a need for a high level programming language, based on common words, that will allow an operator to generate all the required programs for the manufacturing floor. The combination of part design, engineering, and process planning is just one aspect of computer aided engineering. This new field is responsible for linking the basic factory operations via a common data base, applying group technology, simulation programming, and advanced technologies.

Information will still be used by humans, in addition to machines. As John Naisbett (1984), author of *Megatrends* suggests, 'Information technology brings order to the chaos of information pollution and therefore gives value to data that would be otherwise useless. If users, through information utilities, can locate the information they need, they will pay for it.' The responsibility of engineers and managers in the future will thus be to effectively locate, interpret, and apply the information available, to enhance manufacturing and to supply the necessary data for continued operations.

Information systems and the service sector

The future challenge to the service sector is to effectively apply technology. With more computers being accepted into society the importance of information science has increased considerably. However, management must be concerned with the operation of equipment and more importantly software, to ensure that the total system is acceptable to users. Information system designers in the future should be concerned with problem solving and management, and with the interface provided to humans. The increased application of automation to the office environment has brought increased concentration on improving ergonomics and workstation design.

Along with the trend to design improved workstations has come the concept of bioware. Bioware can be thought of as the area of biological interpretation of data; in other words how will the human do it? This area of development is responsible for the term 'user friendly', and has resulted in improving the human-computer interface.

The nature of traditional information jobs, such as accounting and finance, have been the leaders in the use of computers within the office environment. Because of increased automation, several traditional jobs will be likely to see diminishing employment. As machines communicate with each other there will be less human involvement, and as may be expected, less opportunity for error. Advances in office automation have seen many changes within the clerical support staff, and have caused concern over areas such as radiation from cathode ray tubes, lighting, physical comfort, and productivity.

The advances in computer technology for office automation will be based on the same devices that have spawned industrial automation; the microprocessors. While computers decrease in size they have been increasing in power, and it is the power that service personnel will use.

Designers are being treated to the advent of the computer aided design station, secretaries to the computer integrated workstation, and factory technicians to portable computers. These devices have revolutionalised these and similar careers and often require workers to have advanced training. When a microprocessor is incorporated into the workstation, the user has gained stand alone power while maintaining a central computer link. This link allows people to free the central computer for more tasks while leaving the routine operation to the workstation control device.

11.5 HUMAN RESOURCE CONSIDERATIONS

As the number of businesses purchasing small computer systems increases, the programmer will become more involved with the production of software. The small business cannot afford a computer service technician, so increasing numbers of technicians will be supported by computer retailers and manufacturers. However, as computers proliferate and grow older a new service industry will evolve; the computer repair shop, similar to today's TV and electronic repair shops.

The focus of computer activities in developed countries will shift from accounting, inventory, and sales functions to production, insurance, health care, and agriculture. As the primary application of computers shifts from accounting to production, the systems analyst will need a stronger background in production operations. Additionally, with the increased use of robotics and industrial automation a fundamental understanding of CAD/CAM will be required.

Today, most computer operating personnel, programmers, and service technicians normally work 40 hours weekly, but not on regular schedules. Programming must sometimes be done according to equipment availability, often at night or at weekends. Repair personnel generally are on call twenty-four hours a day according to various schedules and rotations. Irregular work schedules for personnel working with computers are likely to increase in the future.

The work environments of these people are clean, comfortable, air-conditioned offices and computer rooms. In the future, computers and personnel will be required to work in the production environment, solving operational problems. This will require experience in both production and operations management (Shell, 1982).

The US Bureau of Labor Statistics suggests the following employment trends:

	1970	*1980*	*1990*
Systems Analyst	100	240	400
Programmers	150	330	500
Operators	120	520	840
Key entry	250	240	220
Technicians	30	85	170

Kurt K. Curtis has written in a National Science Foundation report (Cotellessa 1983) 'there is a shortage of computer manpower which is expected to persist for the foreseeable future, but only the educational institutions have a real crisis'. Factors which support this conclusion include:

1. Graduate students pursuing fields aligned with business/industrial employment versus education
2. Loss of faculty to business/industry is twice as high as any other discipline
3. Lower enrolment in Engineering disciplines
4. University funding cuts

Faculty mobility has been influenced by both working conditions and salary. Students with relevant experience have been able to substantially increase their income upon graduation. In the US several universities have attempted to adjust to demand, 80 per cent have increased loads, 50 per cent have increased course offerings, and 66 per cent utilise more graduate assistants in an increased capacity. All of these measures make teaching less attractive and have the long term effect of discouraging new prospects. Teaching must be made more attractive and salaries raised for real improvement to occur.

As the focus of computer work shifts to production, insurance or other new fields, experience and education in these fields will be required. This means that the computer expert who expects to succeed in production will need both production and computer experience.

A recent trend is for the computer specialist to move upward in management, instead of being tied to the computer room. This will require additional management skills and experience for these technical people.

The following conclusions can be drawn with regards to employment and education in computer related fields:

1. The computer eliminates clerical jobs but creates higher level technical jobs. This causes some job displacement, because new openings require more skill and education.
2. As the number of working women increase in the total worker population, the number of women working in the computer field will also increase.
3. Enrolment in computer-related college/university courses is increasing.

4. Professionals engaged in design will concentrate on software conversion to hardware, communications, and whole office systems. Development of workplace modules combining work surfaces, seating, telephone, telex, computer terminal, microcomputer, and photocopier will emerge.
5. MIS will become more cost effective and more relevant to decision-making. Until very recently, computers have been of little help in decision-making. This is probably because systems analysts have little experience in decision-making and because decision-making is more of an art than a science (Martin and Shell, 1980).

As system analysts learn how to assist top management in the decision process their status within the organisation will likely increase. Thirty years ago, the original marketing approach utilised for selling computers was based on reduced manpower, however the opposite was most often true. The current approach stresses processing and information capabilities. The future challenge to computer experts is to reduce the paper flood, to provide timely, pertinent information to improve the efficiency of the organisation, realise better decision-making, and increase profitability.

11.6 EPILOGUE

The computerised information age is upon us. There are going to be more people involved in information jobs than ever before and more people will be required to be computer literate.

Technology is changing very rapidly. New and more powerful computer systems are developing. However, it is the area of software development which will see the most growth. Areas such as artificial intelligence and parallel processing are critical components for the factory of the future. The level of processing required for factory automation will need extensive computer power and real time response. This can be accomplished by linking series of microprocessor chips, programmable controllers, and computers together in a common network.

Other changes will be occurring in equipment design and sophistication through human factors and advances in microprocessor programming. New technologies will end the reign of the cathode ray tube for display, the keyboard for input, and paper for output. New systems will begin to operate in higher level computer languages and eventually, natural language. There is also a move to interpretive languages, which do not require a compiler. Many of the basic language systems which operate on present day microcomputers are of this type. New advances in chip technologies will see increased processing speeds and more complex designs through VLSI.

The information age will signify many changes for all peoples throughout the world. It will be an exciting time and we are a part of it. The future holds success for those individuals who will be able to fully utilise tomorrow's computers and information technologies.

References

Bureau of Labor Statistics Department of Commerce, US Government Printing Office.

COTELLESSA, R. F. (1983) (Chairman), *Report of the Information Technology Workshop*, National Science Foundation, October.

DAVIS, A. L. (1983) 'Computer Architecture', *IEEE Spectrum*, November, pp. 94–9.

DEAN, N. (1983) 'Reflections on Artificial Intelligence', *Personal Computing*, June.

DOUGLAS, R. J. (1983) 'Need and Uses', *IEEE Spectrum*, November, pp. 41–5.

EDEN, R. C., LIVINGSTON, A. R., and WELCH, B. M. (1983) 'Integrated Circuits the Case for Gallium Arsenide', *IEEE Spectrum*, December, pp. 30–7.

KANADE, T. and REDDY, R. (1983) 'Computer Vision: The Challenge of Imperfect Inputs', *IEEE Spectrum*, November, pp. 88–91.

MARTIN, D. D. and R. L. SHELL (1980) *What Every Engineer Should Know About Human Resource Management* (New York: Marcel Dekker).

NAISBETT, J. (1984) *Megatrends*, (Warner Books).

SHELL, R. L. (1982) 'The Impact of Automation on Work Measurement', *Proceedings, Fall Industrial Engineering Conference*, Institute of Industrial Engineers, pp. 348–53.

SHELL, R. L. and N. A. DAMACHI (1983) 'Managing the Industrial Engineering Function in Developing Countries: The Role of IE', *Proceedings, Annual Industrial Engineering Conference*, Institute of Industrial Engineers, pp. 383–92.

SHELL, R. L. and O. G. OKOGBAA (1983) 'The Effect of Mental Fatigue on Knowledge Worker Performance', *Proceedings, Fall Industrial Engineering Conference*, Institute of Industrial Engineers, pp. 631–8.

WALTZ, D. L. (1983) 'Helping Computers Understand Natural Languages', *IEEE Spectrum*, November, pp. 81–4.

Index